Steck-Vaughn

Think-Alongs™

Comprehending As You Read

Level C

Teacher's Edition

Program Authors

Senior Author
Roger Farr

Co-Authors
Jennifer Conner
Elizabeth Haydel
Bruce Tone
Beth Greene
Tanja Bisesi
Cheryl Gilliland

STECK-VAUGHN
ELEMENTARY · SECONDARY · ADULT · LIBRARY

A Harcourt Company

www.steck-vaughn.com

Acknowledgments

Editorial Director	Diane Schnell
Project Editor	Anne Souby
Associate Director of Design	Cynthia Ellis
Design Manager	Ted Krause
Production and Design	Julia Miracle-Hagaman
Photo Editor	Claudette Landry
Product Manager	Patricia Colacino
Cover Design	Ted Krause
Cover Sculpture	Lonnie Springer
Cover Production	Alan Klemp

Think-Alongs™ is a trademark of Steck-Vaughn Company.

ISBN 0-7398-0091-4

3 4 5 6 7 8 9 0 PO 03 02 01

Contents

Program Overview

We have all had the experience of reading a page and then not remembering what we read. For those of us who are good readers, this experience only occurs once in a while, when we are distracted and thinking about something else. But for newer readers or poor readers, this experience occurs repeatedly. They read the words on the page without making connections or visualizing what they are reading. They *are* reading, but they are not comprehending. For these students, and for all of us at times, it can be too easy to read the words on the page without thinking about the meaning of those words.

How can you encourage students to think while they read?

The **Steck-Vaughn Think-Alongs™: Comprehending As You Read** series is designed to provide you with a tool to do just that. In this series, students will learn to engage in a process called "thinking along." Whether students are thinking aloud or responding to written questions, the activities in this series will help them think as they read. By practicing the strategies presented here, students will become better comprehenders of the variety of texts they will encounter in school, in testing situations, and in their personal lives. These reading comprehension and critical thinking strategies will help students understand all texts, both expository and narrative, and help them feel successful about reading.

The **Steck-Vaughn Think-Alongs: Comprehending As You Read** series is designed to provide opportunities for students to:

- Think and comprehend as they read.
- Learn the reading strategies needed to become more effective comprehenders.
- Practice effective reading strategies with a variety of texts.
- Construct meaning as they read.
- Become more effective in their use of metacognitive reading strategies.
- Connect what they know to what is being read.
- Develop techniques that promote more effective reading.
- Write while reading, thus encouraging them to think about the text.
- Discuss the story and internalize unfamiliar vocabulary.
- Learn to use ideas developed while reading to write more effectively.
- Practice thinking strategies that can be used to improve reading comprehension test-taking skills.

The activities in this book are designed to work with your classroom goals and schedule. The activities are flexible and can be adjusted to suit your students' needs and your personal teaching style. The program provides a way for you to model the think-along process for students by using the "Introducing Thinking Along" section on pages T12–T15. The student books are easy to use, and the teacher's edition provides numerous activities for introducing, discussing, and extending each of the selections.

About the Author

Dr. Roger Farr, program author of **Steck-Vaughn Think-Alongs: Comprehending As You Read**, has been working on the strategies in this program for more than a decade. He has conducted hundreds of workshops and seminars with teachers over the years, has been directly involved with students in applying these strategies, and has received feedback from many teachers who have used the techniques in their classrooms. Dr. Farr has applied this research to **Think-Alongs**, thus developing effective and easy-to-use strategies for both teaching and learning reading comprehension.

A teacher of kindergarten through graduate school, Dr. Farr is a senior author of *Signatures* and *Collections*, both K-6 reading programs from Harcourt School Publishers, and he also serves as a special consultant to Harcourt on assessment and measurement. He is Chancellors' Professor of Education and Director of the Center for Innovation in Assessment at Indiana University.

Dr. Farr is a former president of the International Reading Association. In 1984, the IRA honored Dr. Farr for outstanding lifetime contributions to the teaching of reading. In the same year, he was elected to the IRA Reading Hall of Fame, and in 1988 he was selected by the IRA as the Outstanding Reading Teacher Educator.

Components

The series consists of six pupil's editions for grades one through six and six accompanying annotated teacher's editions, as well as a video simulating actual classroom use.

Pupil's Editions

The pupil's editions are divided into four units in Levels A–C and three units in Levels D–F. Each unit of three selections introduces and then provides practice for a specific reading comprehension strategy. In the first selection, students answer questions related to that specific strategy as they read. In the second and third selections, students are asked strategy questions as well as an increasing number of open-ended questions. This scaffolding approach helps students apply various reading comprehension strategies as they read. The write-in boxes and the scaffolding approach provide structure and organization for students. The questions are different from many traditional reading questions in that there are no correct or incorrect responses. Students are encouraged to think about the text in their own way.

In addition, the pupil's editions include two sections that allow students to apply the think-along process to test-taking situations. These sections consist of three reading passages including think-along questions followed by multiple-choice and short-answer questions modeled after standardized tests. A purpose-setting question leads students to focus. These practice sections help improve students' test-taking skills.

Pupil's Edition Features

Strategies for thinking along are introduced and modeled. Students are given ample practice thinking along with real literature and then responding in writing.

The pupil's edition includes:

- **Introduction to the Strategy**
- **Reading Selection with Write-in Boxes**
- **Writing Activity**
- **Test-Taking Practice**

Introduction to the Strategy

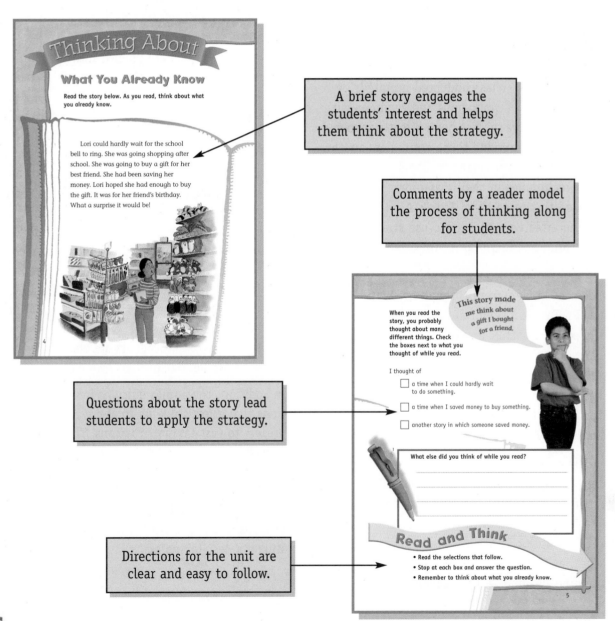

Thinking About

What You Already Know

Read the story below. As you read, think about what you already know.

Lori could hardly wait for the school bell to ring. She was going shopping after school. She was going to buy a gift for her best friend. She had been saving her money. Lori hoped she had enough to buy the gift. It was for her friend's birthday. What a surprise it would be!

4

A brief story engages the students' interest and helps them think about the strategy.

Comments by a reader model the process of thinking along for students.

This story made me think about a gift I bought for a friend.

When you read the story, you probably thought about many different things. Check the boxes next to what you thought of while you read.

I thought of

☐ a time when I could hardly wait to do something.

☐ a time when I saved money to buy something.

☐ another story in which someone saved money.

What else did you think of while you read?

Questions about the story lead students to apply the strategy.

Read and Think

- Read the selections that follow.
- Stop at each box and answer the question.
- Remember to think about what you already know.

5

Directions for the unit are clear and easy to follow.

Reading Selection

Save the River!
By Sarah Glasscock

This selection is about a boy named Vince. He lives in the future with his computer named Jane. They go back in time to help save a river. Read the selection to find out how they try to save the river.

A River in Trouble

It was the year 2097. Vince was floating on his back in the clear water of the San Carlos River. His computer named Jane was waving from the shore.

1 What do you think about a computer that can wave from the shore?

> The **Let's Read** section introduces the selection and sets the purpose for reading.

"Jane, would you show me what this river looked like one hundred years ago?" Vince asked.

"Sure. Why do you want to see it as it was back then?" asked Jane.

"I'd just like to know if the river was this beautiful then," said Vince.

2 What are you thinking about now?

> Questions in the boxes throughout the selections encourage students to take "think breaks" as they read. These questions reinforce the strategies.

Soon Jane's screen lit up. There was a picture of the river as it had looked one hundred years ago. Jane made the picture bigger so Vince could see it.

Vince looked closely and saw a man and his son fishing. "Maybe that's my great-great grandfather!"

Jane quickly searched her computer memory. "That could be. You did have relatives here at that time."

"There were so many animals that came to the river back then," Jane said. "The San Carlos has been giving them food and water for hundreds of years."

A few feet away, Vince saw a deer drinking from the river. "It still does. The river hasn't changed. That's amazing. I wonder why the river hasn't changed."

> Full-color art or photos support the text and draw the reader into the text.

Writing Activity

Time to Write!

Vince and Jane went back in time to help save a river. You know that problems cannot be solved with help from the future.

• For this activity, you will write a letter to the mayor about a problem in your city. Tell how you can help solve the problem.

Prewriting

First, name three problems. Tell how you can help solve them.

Problem: _____

How I can help solve the problem: _____

Problem: _____

How I can help solve the problem: _____

Problem: _____

How I can help solve the problem: _____

... of the problems.
... et of paper to write
... the mayor about it.

125

> The **Time to Write!** page provides a writing prompt as well as a prewriting activity for a variety of writing experiences, including letters, reports, essays, journal entries, and directions.

Test-Taking Practice

Thinking Along on Tests

You have been thinking along as you read. Now practice thinking along to help you answer test questions.

Read and Think

• Read each selection.
• Stop at each box and answer the question.
• Answer the questions at the end of each selection.

Why do bats have a bad name?

Bats have a bad name! Bats look scary to some people. Bats also can fly, but they are not birds. They are the only mammals that can fly. Some people are afraid that bats will get caught in their hair. Bats do not try to do that. Some people think bats will bite them. Bats almost never bite a person.

1 What are you thinking about now?

132

Darken the circle for the correct answer.

1. The writer thinks that people should _____.
   Ⓐ get rid of all bats
   Ⓑ stop reading about vampires
   Ⓒ learn to like bats
   Ⓓ live in caves

2. Some people are afraid that bats will bite and _____.
   Ⓐ get caught in their hair
   Ⓑ eat too many insects
   Ⓒ hurt their ponds
   Ⓓ harm crops

3. One fact about bats is that they _____.
   Ⓐ try to bite people
   Ⓑ sleep during the day
   Ⓒ are birds
   Ⓓ cannot fly

4. Bats help people because they _____.
   Ⓐ live only in caves
   Ⓑ like to scare people
   Ⓒ have to drink water
   Ⓓ eat many insects

Write your answer on the lines below.

5. What is one way people can help bats?

_____
_____
_____

135

> Test-taking practice sections help students apply the think-along concept to standardized test-taking situations.

> Students are given both multiple-choice and short-answer questions as standardized test-taking practice.

Teacher's Edition

The teacher's edition provides suggestions for introducing each strategy as well as a lesson plan for each selection. The teacher's edition also includes reduced pupil pages with possible student responses and suggestions for how to interpret and react to those responses. These suggestions indicate the strategies that the student responses reflect.

Highlighted throughout the teacher's edition are three types of additional activities:

- **ESOL** activities include suggestions for helping students whose first language is not English apply the think-along strategies.
- **Meeting Individual Needs** activities address the needs of students with different learning styles.
- **Reinforcing the Strategies** helps students maintain previously learned strategies.

In addition, pages T12–T15 of the teacher's edition include directions for how to model the think-along process by thinking aloud so students can think along. Part of this demonstration includes coached practice for students.

Blackline Masters

The teacher's edition contains several blackline masters:

- Three stories to use with the optional teacher modeling section. (Note: When duplicating these masters for classroom use, adjust the setting on the photocopy machine so that the suggestions for teacher-directed questions in color will not reproduce on the student pages. Or, you may cover up these suggestions with a strip of paper when you photocopy these pages so they will not reproduce.)

- A letter to parents or caregivers in both English and Spanish to inform them of the program and provide suggestions for interacting with their children to increase reading comprehension.
- A self-assessment master that students can complete after they finish each selection. This evaluative tool helps students focus on metacognition and their attitudes about the think-along process.
- A scoring rubric for you to track students' progress in thinking along.

Video

A video accompanying the program features an introduction to the think-along process by Roger Farr and shows the program in use in actual classroom settings at several grade levels. It serves as a staff development tool for inservice or training purposes.

Teacher's Edition Features

The teacher's edition provides a wealth of information to enhance students' interaction with text through reading, writing, and discussion. At a glance, teachers can see a reduced pupil page. The program allows minimal preparation time and offers suggestions for maximizing instruction.

The teacher's edition features:

- *Before Reading Activities*
- *Possible Responses*
- *Helpful Tips*
- *After Reading Activities*

Before reading activities include:

- a clearly stated strategy,
- a summary of the selection for quick reference,
- a vocabulary list of unfamiliar words or words critical to understanding,
- suggestions for introducing the selection, and
- the purpose for reading.

Possible student responses demonstrate what to watch for and how to determine which strategies are being used. Questions are provided to further enhance student learning.

Helpful suggestions for meeting the individual needs of students, including those whose first language is not English, are given throughout the selections.

After reading activities include:

- suggestions for leading a discussion of what students write in the boxes. Such a discussion is a critical step in the think-along process,
- suggestions for reteaching the strategy to give additional options for student learning.

Each selection includes a list of additional activities and books on the topic to provide resources for further student interaction.

The writing section identifies ways for students to share what they have written.

Research Supporting Think-Along Strategies

Research during the past several decades has demonstrated that when students interact with text while reading, reading comprehension has improved. The impact of response techniques has been demonstrated in research involving reciprocal teaching, comprehension monitoring, think-aloud strategies, and writing in response to reading.

Do oral and written think-along activities help students understand what they are reading?

Ample research evidence demonstrates that active reasoning while reading enhances reading comprehension. Research has demonstrated the positive effects on reading comprehension when teachers ask thought-provoking questions while students are learning to read and when reading increasingly difficult new texts. Finally, numerous studies have demonstrated that good readers are active thinkers while reading.

Davey, Beth. **Think aloud—modeling the cognitive process of reading comprehension.** *Journal of Reading*, 27 (1), October 1983, pp. 44-47.

Kucan, Linda and Isabel L. Beck. **Four fourth graders thinking aloud: an investigation of genre effects**, *Journal of Literacy Research*, 28 (2), June 1996, pp. 259-287.

Loxterman, Jane. A, Isabel L. Beck, and Margaret G. McKeown. **The effects of thinking aloud during reading on students' comprehension of more or less coherent text.** *Reading Research Quarterly*, 29 (4), October-December 1994, pp. 352-367.

Pressley, Michael and Peter Afflerbach. *Verbal Protocols of Reading: The Nature of Constructively Responsive Reading.* Hillsdale, NJ: Lawrence Erlbaum Associates, 1995.

Does verbal or written interaction before and after reading enhance a reader's comprehension?

The research literature has documented the importance of a reader's active interaction with text—not only during reading, but also before and after reading. Readers who read with a purpose and discuss, write, and draw in active response to text are significantly better comprehenders than those who are passive readers.

McMahon, Susan I. and Taffy E. Raphael. *The Book Club Connection.* New York: Teachers' College Press, 1997.

Ogle, Donna. **Developing problem solving through language arts instruction.** In Collins, Cathy and John N. Mangieri (Eds.) *Teaching Thinking: An Agenda for the Twenty-First Century.* Hillsdale, NJ: Lawrence Erlbaum Associates, 1992, pp. 25-39.

Palincsar, Annemarie Sullivan and Ann L. Brown. **Reciprocal teaching of comprehension—fostering and comprehension monitoring activities.** *Cognition and Instruction*, 1 (2), 1984, pp. 117-125.

Does being aware of reading strategies help a reader comprehend more effectively and easily?

Awareness of reading strategies and how one is comprehending is called metacognition. The research on the positive impact of metacognitive strategies on reading comprehension is well documented.

Baker, Linda and Ann L. Brown. **Metacognitive skills and reading.** In Pearson, David P. (Ed.) *Handbook of Reading Research.* New York: Longman, 1984, pp. 353-394.

Farr, Roger, et al. **Writing in response to reading.** *Educational Leadership*, 47 (6), March 1990, pp. 66-69.

Paris, Scott G., Barbara A. Wasik, and Gert Van der Westhuizen. **Meta-metacognition: a review of research on metacognition and reading.** In Readence, John E. et al. (Eds.) *Dialogues in Literacy Research: Thirty-seventh Yearbook of The National Reading Conference*, National Reading Conference, 1988, pp. 143-166.

Raphael, Taffy E. and Clydie A. Wonnacott. **Heightening fourth-grade students' sensitivity to sources of information for answering comprehension questions.** *Reading Research Quarterly*, 20 (3), Spring 1985, pp. 282-296.

Tips for Using Think-Alongs in Your Classroom

An important aspect of using **Think-Alongs** in your classroom is to monitor and discuss students' responses to the questions in the boxes. The following tips will help you encourage and direct students in using **Think-Alongs**.

- Give positive feedback as you walk around the room and look at student responses.

- Check that students are responding to the questions in the boxes. If they cannot answer the question, have them write whatever they are thinking.

- If students are unable to write an answer to the question, encourage them to draw a picture. This is a particularly good strategy to use with students whose primary language is not English.

- Assure students that there are no wrong answers. Answers will vary because students are making their own connections with the text.

- Encourage students to write their ideas in the boxes fairly quickly and then continue reading the selection.

- The amount students write is not important. They do not have to write complete sentences.

- Spelling, grammar, and punctuation are not as important as thinking and responding.

- Students may use a variety of strategies as they respond to questions.

- If students write answers that are not clearly related to the selection, follow up by asking them why they wrote what they did.

- If students do not understand the meaning of a word, have them figure it out from the context, or have them keep a list of words to look up. Provide help when needed.

- For a student who struggles with the process, model for that student at a specific place in the selection.

Scoring the Tests

Scoring the tests can tell you how well your students are learning to use the think-along strategies. For each test, score 1 point for each multiple-choice question correct (total 12) and 2 points for each open-ended response (total 6). Add the two for a total of up to 18 points for the test. Refer to the chart below for how to interpret the raw score.

Interpreting Test Scores

Raw Score	Letter Grade	Number Grade
16–18	A	90–100
13–15	B	80–89
10–12	C	70–79
Below 10	D	Below 70

Planning Further Instruction

Scores of 90 or above are excellent. These students are good readers and should be encouraged to continue independent reading. The students are probably thinking extensively while they read. Occasional practice in the think-along strategies, especially as new content area materials and new genres are introduced, would be worthwhile.

Scores of 70 to 90 fall in a range of good to satisfactory. These students need to continue to write what they are thinking as they read. Discussing with students what they have written will be helpful to strengthen their comprehending strategies. These students will also profit from the introduction of these strategies with different reading genres and content areas.

Scores below 70 are unsatisfactory. It would be useful for these students to work in small groups with you using the suggestions on pages T12–T15. Teacher modeling as well as encouraging student oral and written responses will help these students use reading strategies more effectively.

The following warm-up activities are optional. Feel free to modify the activities to meet your teaching goals and students' needs. These activities introduce your students to what it means to think along while reading. These activities will be valuable for all of your students, but especially for those who have difficulties comprehending what they read.

Activity 1
Modeling

Think aloud so your students can think along!

Read the Story Aloud

"Pedro put craft sticks together to make toy airplanes."

First, model thinking along with your students by thinking aloud while you read. Use the story "Pedro's Planes" (Master 1 on pages T16–T19). Duplicate enough copies so that each student has one. Throughout the story you will find suggestions of what to say at certain points in the text. (Note: When duplicating these masters for classroom use, adjust the setting on the photocopy machine so that the text in color will not reproduce on the student pages. Or, you may cover up the text in color with a strip of paper so it will not reproduce on the student pages.)

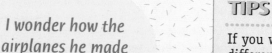

I wonder how the airplanes he made looked.

TIPS

If you want to use a different story or substitute your own statements to model thinking along, keep these tips in mind:

- Think aloud every five or six sentences.
- Use a variety of strategies when you think aloud.
- Think aloud only at the end of a sentence, not in the middle of a sentence.

Activity 2
Providing Coached Practice

Get students to think along by asking specific questions.

Next, have students start thinking along with a story. Read the story "A Visit to the Farm" (Master 2 on pages T20–T24) aloud to students. You may duplicate copies for your students.

Again, photocopy the pages so that the type in color does not reproduce on the student pages. Stop at the points marked in the story and call on individual students to answer the questions provided in the text.

Read the Story Aloud

"Candy was the gentlest horse Beth had ever been on."

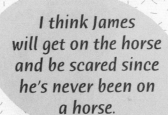

What do you think might happen next?

I think James will get on the horse and be scared since he's never been on a horse.

TIPS

In "A Visit to the Farm," places are marked to ask these questions:

- What do you think might happen next?
- What does this remind you of?
- What are you picturing in your mind?

Activity 3
Providing More Coached Practice

Get students to think along by asking, "What are you thinking about now?"

Next, have students think along by asking them the more general question, "What are you thinking about now?" Read the story "A Camping Adventure" (Master 3 on pages T25–T28) aloud to students.

You may duplicate copies for your students. (Photocopy the pages so the type in color does not reproduce.) Stop at the points marked in the story and call on individual students to answer the questions provided in the text.

Read the Story Aloud

"It's nothing," Ashley said. "Just the rain hitting the leaves of the trees."

What are you thinking about now?

I'm thinking about the time my family went camping. The noises at night scared me.

TIPS

- If a student has trouble answering the general "What are you thinking about now" question, ask a more specific question, such as "What might happen next?"

- Have several students tell you what they are thinking about each time you stop.

- After a few students have shared their thoughts, share your own as well.

Activity 4
Reflecting

Get students to reflect on their responses and on the process of thinking along.

Next, have students think about their responses to the questions and how they feel about the process of thinking along. Respond to students' answers in a positive way, but if their answers seem unrelated to the reading, ask for clarification. Point out the strategies they are using. Note the individual approaches they are taking to show that many different answers are acceptable.

Finally, ask students how they feel about using the think-along process.

What do you think about the think-along process?

Thinking along is great! It makes me stop and think about the story in different ways. That really helps me to understand it better.

TIPS

To get students to support their responses:

- "That's an interesting idea. What made you think of that?"
- "I think I know what you mean. Can you explain a little more?"
- "I never thought of that. What made you think of that?"
- "I like that idea. Where did it come from?"

To get students to diversify their responses:

- "What an interesting idea! No one else thought of that."
- "Who else has another way of thinking about the story?"

To get students to use different strategies:

- "What do you think will happen next?"
- "What does the story remind you of?"
- "What picture does this make in your mind?"

Pedro's Planes

Pedro wanted to be a pilot when he grew up. He thought about airplanes all the time. He read books about airplanes from the library. He drew pictures of airplanes in art class. He put craft sticks together to make toy airplanes.

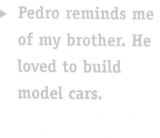

I wonder how the planes he made looked.

So no one had to guess what Pedro had all over the room he shared with his older brother Luis.

There were model airplanes, of course. Luis called the room "Pedro's hangar." Pedro had made many of the models. His dad and Luis helped him build some of them.

Pedro reminds me of my brother. He loved to build model cars.

Pedro was always looking at catalogs of toy airplanes. He would save his money until he could afford ones that he liked the most.

One day Luis saw Pedro looking at a catalog for a long time. He noticed that Pedro was not turning the pages. He looked over Pedro's shoulder. There was a picture of a toy airplane that looked very real. It was called the "Red Hot Flyer." ....▶ I bet he wants to get the "Red Hot Flyer."

Behind the plane was what looked like a toy building. "You have a plane almost like that, Pedro."

"Yes," Pedro said. "But I don't have an airport. I could put this plane and lots of my other planes around this airport."

Pedro knew what Luis was going to ask. "Where are you going to put all that, Pedro?"

"Over there on that table," Pedro said. "We would just need to move that lamp." ....▶ He's not going to have room for anything but airplanes.

Luis shook his head and smiled. "Okay," he said, checking the price of the plane in the catalog. He was surprised that it didn't cost more since it was supposed to come with its own airport.

Weeks later Pedro was very excited. He had sent away for his "Red Hot Flyer." He expected it and the airport to arrive any day!

Luis had helped Pedro clear the table for the airport. When the package arrived, Luis looked worried. How did the plane and the airport fit in that small package? ....▶ I wonder what might be missing?

Pedro's face became long and sad as he opened the box. He was sure there was a mistake. There was no airport inside. He looked at all the parts carefully. They all belonged to the plane.

> I think the company just forgot it.

Luis got out the catalog. "It doesn't say that the plane comes with an airport," he said.

"It shows the airport!" Pedro said.

"I guess that's just for show," Luis said. Luis looked all through the catalog. "I don't see that airport being sold anywhere," he said.

> I would be very disappointed if I didn't get something I expected.

Pedro was very disappointed. He laid the parts for the plane aside. It lay on the empty table for several days. Then one day, Luis came into the room carrying a bunch of flattened cardboard boxes. He also had tape, paint, and other supplies. He laid them all out on the table.

"What's going on, Luis?" Pedro said.

> I think Luis is going to make an airport.

"We're going to make an airport!" Luis said. Pedro frowned. How could these old boxes make an airport?

Luis propped the catalog up in front of them. It was open to the picture of the plane and the airport. In a few hours, Pedro began to see how the boxes could be turned into an airport. A small terminal building was taking shape. Pedro was busy making a hangar, and Luis painted the terminal white.

Eventually the terminal had windows with people waiting at them.

Pedro was very excited! It was going to be a wonderful airport! Luis added more buildings. "Those aren't in the picture," Pedro said. ....

They are making a better airport than the one in the catalog!

"So what," Luis said. "We can have a better airport than they show there."

Luis had never before been so interested in Pedro's plane collection. Each night they would finish supper, do dishes, and look at each other. "Time to go up and work on *our* airport!" Luis would say. ....

They're probably having fun working together.

A Visit to the Farm

James had been at the farm for only a couple of hours, but his cousin Beth already knew there was going to be trouble.

"Want to go to the pond and fish?" she asked him.

"Fish?" James asked. "You mean like use a net or something?"

"No," Beth said. "I've got poles and worms."

"Worms," James said. "No thanks." He knew this family vacation with his relatives in the country was going to be a bust. First thing that happens—they're offering him worms! Already he missed the city. He wondered what the guys were doing at the park. They probably were playing football.

What do you think might happen next?

Beth showed James the pond. She didn't bother to take the fishing poles.

"What kind of fish do you catch here?" James asked, wrinkling his nose.

Beth tried not to notice the tone of his voice. "Catfish," she said. "Some of them are almost as big as whales. Want to go up to the barn now?" she asked.

"I guess so," James said. They slid open the creaky old door. "This place smells weird," he said. He almost looked interested, though. "You actually have a cow in here!" .... What does this remind you of?

"Where else would we get our milk?" Beth asked.

James turned up his nose. "At the grocery store!" he cried. "Where else?"

From around a corner, there came a loud whinny.

"You have a horse?" James asked. Now he seemed interested. He thought of his friend Karl, who rode through the neighborhood on Shasta, the police horse. Karl let James feed Shasta carrots and sugar cubes. .... What are you picturing in your mind?

"We have two horses," Beth said. "Do you want to go for a ride?"

"Yeah!" James said, without thinking. Then he thought about it for a minute. "Well, maybe sometime this week." He had never ridden a horse. He didn't want Beth to know that. What if he fell off?

"Okay," Beth said. "We can go riding when you want." She knew right away that James had never been on a horse. She could tell by the look on his face when she asked if he wanted to go.

She wouldn't push it. She didn't want to embarrass him. If he decided to go, she would let him ride Candy. Candy was the gentlest horse Beth had ever been on, and the horse was very easy to ride.

What do you think might happen next?

The next day they were sitting on the porch, trying to think of something to do. "Could we go to the mall or something?" James asked.

"We don't have a mall in town," Beth said, smiling. "We have a great ice cream store, though."

"You must be kidding," James said. "No mall?" But he began thinking about the ice cream. The milk from the cow hadn't tasted bad at all when it was cold.

What does this remind you of?

"We can hike to town," Beth said. "It's only a mile."

The mile seemed like fifty miles to James, but the ice cream was worth it. He couldn't believe how big and delicious the ice cream cones had been, but walking across the fields was hard work. "I wish we had ridden the horses," he said.

"I never bring the horses to town," Beth said. "But I could saddle them up, and we could ride them around the farm."

James didn't answer.

"I'll put the saddles on them," Beth said. "And I'll show you how to get on," she added. ········▶ What do you think might happen next?

"Okay," James said. He could tell she knew he didn't know how to ride a horse. But since it was the only thing to do out here in the country, he might as well let her show him how. It might be almost as good as playing ball with his friends.

James watched carefully as Beth stood up on a box and put the blankets and saddles on the horses. Then he watched as she put her foot in a stirrup and swung up onto Felix. Felix was smaller than Candy, so it seemed to James that Beth was giving him the better horse.

Then he tried to get on. He had a bit of trouble getting up at first. Beth was tempted to help him, but she didn't. Candy looked at Beth as though she were saying, "Will this city boy be okay?" ··········▶ What are you picturing in your mind?

Beth showed James how to grab hold of a strap on the saddle. On his third try he was up and in the saddle. He had never felt so tall!

Beth led the way slowly. James rocked gently in the saddle as Candy followed Felix. "Giddyup," he commanded. Candy looked back at him with big, dark eyes. This was fun! He was actually riding a horse. Wait till he got home and told Karl and his friends at the park! ·········▶ What do you think will happen next?

"Candy is really a nice horse!" he said.

"She likes you," Beth said. "I can tell."

After that they rode several times every day. Beth showed him how to handle the reins so that he could get Candy to move a little faster.

When the week was over, James had mixed feelings. He was eager to get back to the city, but he was really sorry to leave Beth and Candy.

"You can come back and visit again anytime," Beth said.

"Thanks," James said, rubbing Candy's nose. "Next time you can show me how to catch a catfish." ⋯⋯⋯⋯⋯⋯⋯⋯⋯⋯⋯⋯⋯⋯⋯⋯▶ What does this remind you of?

A Camping Adventure

It was Ashley's idea. She and her sister, Teresa, would borrow their friend's tent and have their "own place" when they went camping with their parents. Teresa liked the idea. She started planning what they could take camping.

"It will be just like our own house," Teresa said. "Only it will be in the woods." ········▷ What are you thinking about now?

"You can't carry too much stuff in your pack!" Ashley said.

"I wasn't planning to take the dollhouse," Teresa said to Ashley. To herself, she thought, "Ashley thinks she knows everything about camping!"

Ashley could put up a tent. That would be a help when it came time to set up camp each night. But she said *no* to every spot that Teresa picked the first evening. Teresa wanted to be off in the woods so it would be more like their own place. She didn't want to be right next to their parent's tent. But this spot was too close to a tree. That spot was on a hill. If it rained, water would get in the tent. ········▷ What are you thinking about now?

Finally, Ashley picked a place that looked good. It was far away from where Mom and Dad put up their tent and cooked the food. After supper, the sisters washed their metal dishes. Ashley tied a pan and a cup to the bottom of her pack.

"What are you doing?" Teresa asked.

"You'll see," Ashley said. ········▷ What are you thinking about now?

They helped Dad put out the fire and went to their tent before it got dark. Ashley threw a long rope up over a low limb on a small tree and tied one end to the straps on her pack. She pulled the other end until the pack was several feet above the ground. Then she tied the rope around the trunk of the tree.

"Why are you doing that?" Teresa asked.

"Bears," Ashley said. She turned away from Teresa to hide her smile. Then she stood on her toes and hit the cup and the pan hanging under her pack. They clanged together. "When they try to get into my pack, that will scare them."

"There aren't bears here. Are there?" Teresa asked.

"Maybe," Ashley said. "Maybe not."

"Even if there were bears," Teresa said, "why would they want your pack?"

"I've got candy bars in there," Ashley said. She jumped up again and banged the cup and pan together.

What are you thinking about now?

That night in the tent, Teresa was glad Ashley knew a lot about camping. She knew about bears.

Soon it began to rain lightly. Teresa couldn't sleep. She heard noises outside the tent. Ashley was sleeping, so Teresa woke her up.

"What's that?" Teresa asked in a whisper.

"What's what?" Ashley said.

"That noise out there."

"It's nothing," Ashley said. "Just the rain hitting the leaves of the trees."

What are you thinking about now?

Ashley went back to sleep. Then Teresa heard the cup and the pan clanking together. The sound sent chills through her body. "The wind isn't blowing that hard!" she thought.

She awakened Ashley. Ashley listened. Something was messing with her pack.

"Bears!" Teresa said.

Ashley giggled. "There are no bears out here," she said. "I was teasing you. It's probably just a raccoon trying to get at my pack. Go back to sleep."

What are you thinking about now?

Teresa tried to sleep. But she kept thinking, "That must be a really tall raccoon."

In the morning, Dad came up to help the girls take down their tent. He wanted to get moving right after breakfast.

"Teresa was afraid of bears last night," Ashley said with a laugh.

"Did you see a bear?" Dad asked.

"Of course not!" Ashley said. She was still laughing quietly. ·········· ▶ What are you thinking about now?

"Well, I wouldn't be surprised if you had," Dad said. "This is a bear's footprint."

Ashley's face turned pale—and then red.

"Gosh, Ashley," Teresa said, "your pan and cup must have scared it away."

That night at their next stop, Ashley and Teresa quickly agreed on a spot for their tent. It was right next to Mom and Dad's. ·········· ▶ What are you thinking about now?

At Home

Dear family of _____ ,

Our class has begun to read stories and articles in a book titled **Think-Alongs™: Comprehending As You Read.** The book uses an approach to reading called "thinking along." Your child will be answering questions as he or she reads, not waiting until the end of the selection to answer questions. In this way, your child will understand and remember better what he or she has read.

You can help your child in many ways. Ask your child about the readings and about the reading strategies he or she is studying in class. Ask how your child feels about thinking along while reading. Read with your child, stopping as you read to discuss the story, such as what has happened and what might happen next.

Encourage your child to think as he or she reads. You will find that he or she will

- comprehend what he or she reads,

- remember it better, and

- enjoy reading more.

Sincerely,

Estimada familia de _____,

Nuestra clase ha comenzado a leer cuentos y artículos de un libro titulado **Think-Alongs™: Comprehending As You Read.** El libro utiliza un enfoque a la lectura llamado "thinking along" (pensar mientras lee). Su niño/a contestará preguntas mientras él o ella lea, sin esperar hasta el final de la selección para responder a las preguntas. En esta forma, su niño/a comprenderá y recordará mejor lo que él o ella haya leído.

Ud. puede ayudar a su niño/a de muchas maneras. Hágale preguntas sobre las lecturas y acerca de las destrezas que está aprendiendo en la clase. Pregúntele cómo se siente mientras piensa cuando está leyendo. Lea con su niño/a, deteniéndose mientras leen para comentar el cuento, y conversar acerca de lo que ha ocurrido y de lo ocurrirá después.

Anime a su niño/a a pensar sobre lo que lee. Ud. se dará cuenta de que él o ella

- comprenderá lo que está leyendo,

- recordará mejor lo que ha leído, y

- disfrutará más de la lectura.

Atentamente,

Thinking About Thinking Along

Read each statement below. Mark the answer that tells how you feel about thinking along as you read.

1. I can write in the boxes when I read.

    True for me.   **Not true for me.**   **I'm not sure.**

2. Writing in the boxes helps me understand what I read.

    True for me.   **Not true for me.**   **I'm not sure.**

3. Writing in the boxes helps me remember what I read.

    True for me.   **Not true for me.**   **I'm not sure.**

4. Writing in the boxes helps me discuss what I read with others.

    True for me.   **Not true for me.**   **I'm not sure.**

Read and answer the question below.

5. Which selection was the most fun to think about when you wrote in the boxes? Why?

_____

_____

_____

_____

_____

_____

Student _____ Date _____

Checklist for Assessing Thinking Along

	RATING				
Not at all				**All the time**	
1	**2**	**3**	**4**	**5**	

How is thinking along working with this student?

1. Is the student able to write in the boxes?   1   2   3   4   5

2. Does the student discuss what he or she wrote in   1   2   3   4   5
the boxes?

3. Can the student support and defend what he or   1   2   3   4   5
she wrote?

4. Does the student use a variety of reading   1   2   3   4   5
comprehension strategies?

5. Does the student seem to understand the selection   1   2   3   4   5
and remember what he or she reads?

6. Does the student pay more attention now to the   1   2   3   4   5
text when he or she reads?

7. How well does the student apply thinking along   1   2   3   4   5
to other subjects?

8. Does the student ask more questions when reading   1   2   3   4   5
in other subject areas?

9. Does the student discuss more about what he or   1   2   3   4   5
she read in other subject areas?

10. Does the student apply reading comprehension   1   2   3   4   5
strategies in other subject areas?

Scope and Sequence

Strategy	Level					
	A	B	C	D	E	F
Retell by drawing pictures	x	x	x	x	x	x
Connect personal experiences	x	x	x	x	x	x
Identify the main idea	x	x	x	x	x	x
Make predictions	x	x	x	x	x	x
Visualize		x	x	x	x	x
Generate questions		x	x	x	x	x
Identify main ideas and details		x	x	x	x	x
Recognize sequence		x	x	x	x	x
Use background knowledge			x	x	x	x
Compare and contrast			x	x	x	x
Make and revise predictions			x	x	x	x
Distinguish between fantasy and reality			x	x	x	x
Identify cause and effect				x	x	x
Summarize				x	x	x
Identify author's purpose				x	x	x
Draw conclusions					x	x
Evaluate and express opinions					x	x
Identify and interpret meaning of figurative language					x	x
Analyze story elements						x
Identify and analyze problems and solutions						x
Evaluate and interpret author's style and technique						x

Strategy Definitions

Level A

Retell by drawing pictures: Students listen to or read a story and then draw one or more pictures to retell the story.

Connect personal experiences: Students recognize similarities between themselves and their lives and the characters and events in the selections they listen to or read independently.

Identify the main idea: Students express the main idea of a selection either in words or in pictures.

Make predictions: Students speculate about what will happen next in a story.

Level B

Visualize: Students try to picture in their heads what they are reading or listening to in a selection.

Generate questions: Students question events, characters, and details as they read.

Identify main ideas and details: Students determine both explicit and implicit main ideas of a selection. They identify details that support the main idea.

Recognize sequence: Students recall events in a selection in the order in which they occur. They also predict what will happen next or what happened prior to the events described in the selection.

Level C

Use background knowledge: Students use what they already know to interpret the ideas in narrative and expository selections.

Compare and contrast: Students compare relationships between events, objects, or characters to see how they are alike and different.

Make and revise predictions: Students speculate about what will happen next in a narrative or expository selection. They confirm or change their predictions based on subsequent information.

Distinguish between fantasy and reality: Students recognize the difference between what could be real and what could not be real.

Level D

Identify cause and effect: Students identify why something happened (cause) and the consequence of an event or action (effect).

Summarize: Students use textual and typographical clues to recognize the organization of expository text. They use the text organization to summarize the selection.

Identify author's purpose: Students understand an author's purpose in writing a particular story or article. They also are able to identify writing for a specific purpose such as to inform, explain, or entertain.

Level E

Draw conclusions: Students use the information provided in a selection to form a conclusion or make inferences about the topic of the selection.

Evaluate and express opinion: Students develop opinions about the subject or content of a selection or evaluate the opinions expressed by the author or character in a selection.

Identify and interpret meaning of figurative language: Students recognize vivid and colorful language that helps to set the mood of a selection or conveys feelings. They interpret the meaning of figurative language.

Level F

Analyze story elements: Students identify and analyze the characters, setting, theme, or plot in a story.

Identify and analyze problems and solutions: Students identify a problem that is stated or implied in a selection and evaluate the solutions presented in the selection.

Evaluate and interpret author's style and technique: Students determine why an author may have written a selection and how the author's writing style and technique makes the selection interesting or unusual.

Annotated Student Pages for

Steck-Vaughn Think-Alongs:
Comprehending As You Read

Thinking About...

What You Already Know

Using Prior Knowledge

Readers use prior knowledge to relate what they already know to what they read. The activities in this unit will help students to apply the strategy of using prior knowledge. Therefore, they will better understand and remember what they read.

Thinking About

What You Already Know

Read the story below. As you read, think about what you already know.

Lori could hardly wait for the school bell to ring. She was going shopping after school. She was going to buy a gift for her best friend. She had been saving her money. Lori hoped she had enough to buy the gift. It was for her friend's birthday. What a surprise it would be!

4

Introducing the Strategy

Choose a story your students have read recently in class. Select a key idea or theme in the story, and ask students what they already knew about this idea before they started to read. You may need to give them some ideas at first. Expand the discussion to talk about different characters and/or events that reminded students of things they already knew as they read. Explain that good readers think about what they already know as they read.

Applying the Strategy

Ask students to follow along as you read the story in the pupil book, or have a volunteer read it. Tell them to think about a time they may have felt as Lori did.

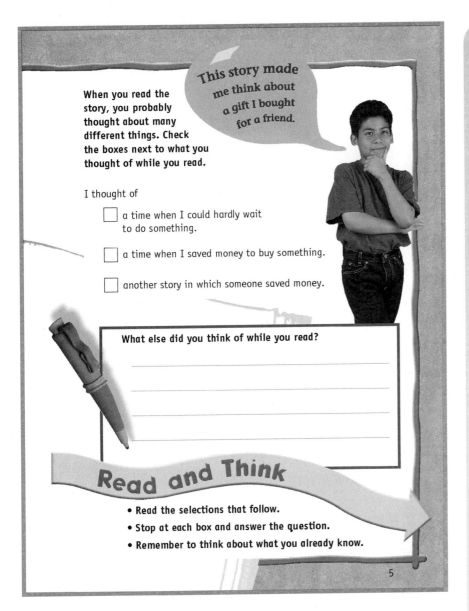

When you read the story, you probably thought about many different things. Check the boxes next to what you thought of while you read.

This story made me think about a gift I bought for a friend.

I thought of

☐ a time when I could hardly wait to do something.

☐ a time when I saved money to buy something.

☐ another story in which someone saved money.

What else did you think of while you read?

_____

_____

_____

_____

Read and Think

- Read the selections that follow.
- Stop at each box and answer the question.
- Remember to think about what you already know.

5

Read and Think

Read the directions so that students know what they are to do in the unit. Explain that they are to answer the questions in the boxes as they read the selections.

- Remind students that answering the questions in the boxes will help them think about the selections.
- Tell them that they can draw a picture to show what they are thinking.
- Encourage them to think about what they already know as they read the selections.

Discussing the Strategy

Have students complete the questions independently or as a group. Ask students what they were thinking about while the story was read. Ask questions such as the following:

- *Have you ever felt the way Lori did?*
- *Did understanding how she felt make the story more interesting?*

Tell students that it is not important if they did not think of all the things in the list following the story. The important thing is that they thought about what they already knew while they were reading.

Explain to students that they will use this strategy as they read the selections in this unit.

Strategy Focus

Using background knowledge to think about a story.

Story at a Glance

Princess Elizabeth outwits a dragon in order to save Prince Ronald.

Vocabulary

You may want to introduce the following words to your students:

expensive   *unfortunately*
fiercest   *magnificent*

Getting Students Started

- **Introducing the Selection**

Introduce the selection by asking students to think about fairy tales they have read. Ask "What are princesses like in these stories?" Tell students that the princess in this story is different from others they may have read about. Call on students to share ideas about how she might be different before they begin reading.

- **Purpose for Reading**

Students read to find out whether Elizabeth is able to save Ronald.

The Paper Bag Princess

By Robert N. Munsch

This selection is about a princess named Elizabeth who tries to save Prince Ronald from a dragon. Read the selection to find out whether Elizabeth is able to save Prince Ronald.

Elizabeth was a beautiful princess. She lived in a castle and had expensive princess clothes. She was going to marry a prince named Ronald.

Unfortunately, a dragon smashed her castle, burned all her clothes with his fiery breath, and carried off Prince Ronald.

 1 What other stories does this story remind you of?

Elizabeth decided to chase the dragon and get Ronald back.

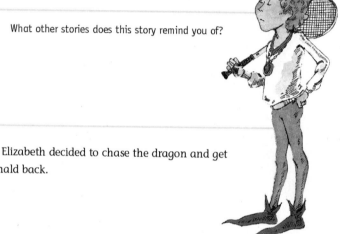

6

Possible Responses
Question 1

Snow White is saved by a prince.

This response indicates that the student is drawing on background knowledge of other fairy tales.

Does Elizabeth marry Prince Ronald?

This student did not answer the question, but was thinking about what might happen later in the story. For this student, you might respond, "That's a great prediction. Now see if you can answer the question. You can write your answer next to your other response."

Dragons aren't real.

Although not responding directly to the question, this student does offer a critical reaction to the text and demonstrates an ability to distinguish fantasy from reality. To encourage a response to the question, ask, "Have you read other make-believe stories about dragons or princesses?"

She looked everywhere for something to wear, but the only thing she could find that was not burnt was a paper bag. So she put on the paper bag and followed the dragon.

He was easy to follow because he left a trail of burnt forests and horses' bones.

Finally, Elizabeth came to a cave with a large door that had a huge knocker on it.

She took hold of the knocker and banged on the door.

2 What do you think might be in the cave?

The dragon stuck his nose out of the door and said, "Well, a princess! I love to eat princesses, but I have already eaten a whole castle today. I am a very busy dragon. Come back tomorrow."

He slammed the door so fast that Elizabeth almost got her nose caught.

Elizabeth grabbed the knocker and banged on the door again.

7

Strategy Tip

Emphasize use of background knowledge—what they know—and can relate to the story.

Possible Responses
Question 2

Ronald?

This response demonstrates that a brief response may be all that is necessary to show that the student is comprehending and thinking about the text as he or she reads.

I don't know.

Remind the student that there is not one right answer, and that it is fine to make a guess about what he or she thinks might be in the cave.

This cave would have to be big to have a big door and a big dragon.

Students often use more than one strategy at a time. This student is not only using background knowledge, but is also visualizing how the cave looks.

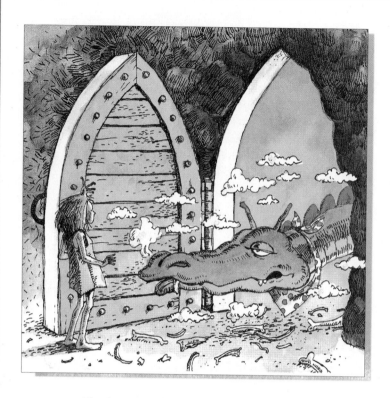

The dragon stuck his nose out of the door and said, "Go away. I love to eat princesses, but I have already eaten a whole castle today. I am a very busy dragon. Come back tomorrow."

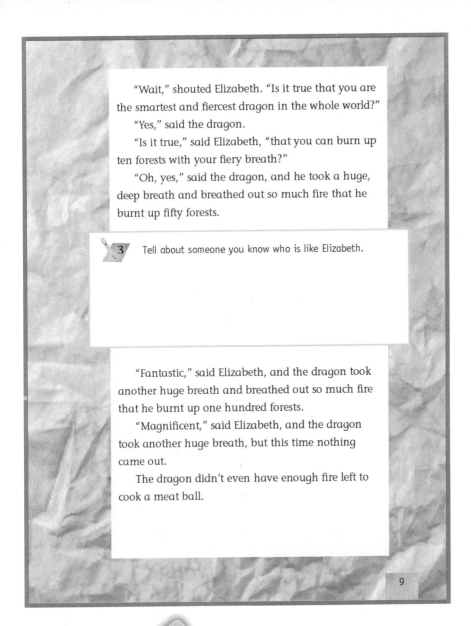

"Wait," shouted Elizabeth. "Is it true that you are the smartest and fiercest dragon in the whole world?"

"Yes," said the dragon.

"Is it true," said Elizabeth, "that you can burn up ten forests with your fiery breath?"

"Oh, yes," said the dragon, and he took a huge, deep breath and breathed out so much fire that he burnt up fifty forests.

3 Tell about someone you know who is like Elizabeth.

"Fantastic," said Elizabeth, and the dragon took another huge breath and breathed out so much fire that he burnt up one hundred forests.

"Magnificent," said Elizabeth, and the dragon took another huge breath, but this time nothing came out.

The dragon didn't even have enough fire left to cook a meat ball.

9

Possible Responses
Question 3

· ·

My friend Katie has nice clothes.

My sister's name is Elizabeth.

Elizabeth is brave like my mom.

This question not only prompts students to use their background knowledge, but it also requires students to compare and contrast.

Elizabeth said, "Dragon, is it true that you can fly around the world in just ten seconds?"

"Why, yes," said the dragon and jumped up and flew all the way around the world in just ten seconds.

He was very tired when he got back, but Elizabeth shouted, "Fantastic, do it again!"

10

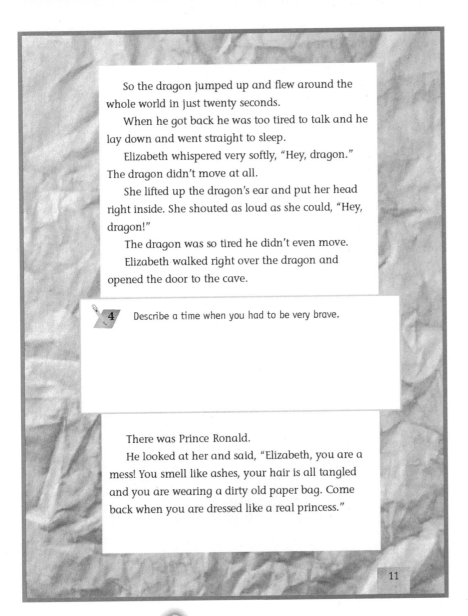

So the dragon jumped up and flew around the whole world in just twenty seconds.

When he got back he was too tired to talk and he lay down and went straight to sleep.

Elizabeth whispered very softly, "Hey, dragon." The dragon didn't move at all.

She lifted up the dragon's ear and put her head right inside. She shouted as loud as she could, "Hey, dragon!"

The dragon was so tired he didn't even move.

Elizabeth walked right over the dragon and opened the door to the cave.

4 Describe a time when you had to be very brave.

There was Prince Ronald.

He looked at her and said, "Elizabeth, you are a mess! You smell like ashes, your hair is all tangled and you are wearing a dirty old paper bag. Come back when you are dressed like a real princess."

11

Possible Responses
Question 4
....

I went to the doctor's office. I was brave.

This response shows that the student is not only using background knowledge, but is also making a connection to personal experience.

My dad found a snake outside. He thought it was dead. He went to pick it up and it moved!

This response demonstrates a use of background knowledge and a connection to personal experience.

Swimming. You could drown.

This response does not directly respond to the question, but is likely prompted by some personal experience or background knowledge. Encourage the student to elaborate by asking, "Did you have to be brave when you were swimming?"

It is very important to have the students read and discuss what they have written in the boxes about what they already know.

Discussing the Think-Alongs

- Give as many students as possible a chance to tell what they wrote in one of the boxes.
- Have students explain what they were thinking when they wrote.
- Ask students how what they already know helps them think about the story.

Reteaching

For those students who have not written or are having difficulty with the activity:

- Ask them to tell what they were thinking about as they read.
- Model your own use of background knowledge by sharing the things you were reminded of as you read.
- Ask questions that prompt students to use background knowledge when thinking about the story, such as the following:
  - *Have you ever been frightened?*
  - *Have you been brave?*
  - *Were you ever surprised by something that happened?*

"Ronald," said Elizabeth, "your clothes are really pretty and your hair is very neat. You look like a real prince, but you are a bum."

They didn't get married after all.

 5   In what ways is Elizabeth not like other princesses?

12

Possible Responses
Question 5

She is smart. Most princesses are dumb. I think this is a good story because it shows that girls are smart and can do anything.

This response demonstrates a very thoughtful understanding of the story, and may get at the author's purpose for having written this twist on the traditional fairy tale.

Princesses wear nice things. Not a paper bag.

This response provides one example of how Elizabeth is different from other princesses. Ask the student to consider other differences or generate a list on the board as students share their responses in the post-reading discussion.

Elizabeth didn't want Prince Ronald because he was not nice.

Sometimes it may be difficult to understand the connection that students are making between the question and the text. Encourage students to elaborate on their responses during discussion after reading. Ask this student, "How do you think she is different from other princesses?"

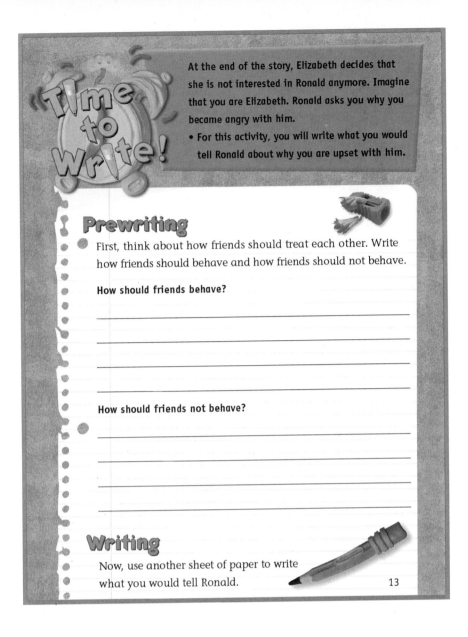

Time to Write!

At the end of the story, Elizabeth decides that she is not interested in Ronald anymore. Imagine that you are Elizabeth. Ronald asks you why you became angry with him.

• For this activity, you will write what you would tell Ronald about why you are upset with him.

Prewriting

First, think about how friends should treat each other. Write how friends should behave and how friends should not behave.

How should friends behave?

_____

_____

_____

_____

How should friends not behave?

_____

_____

_____

_____

Writing

Now, use another sheet of paper to write what you would tell Ronald.

13

Making Connections

Activity Links

• Help students make paper bag puppets and put on their own puppet version of the story.
• Have students illustrate and discuss their favorite folk and fairy tales.
• Have students make up their own versions of favorite fairy tales to share with the class.

Reading Links

You might want to include these books in a discussion of fairy tales with a twist: *Grow Up, Peter Pan!* by Alvin Granowsky (Steck-Vaughn, 1993). *That Awful Cinderella* by Alvin Granowsky (Steck-Vaughn, 1993). *The Frog Prince Continued* by Jon Scieszka (Viking Penguin, 1991). *The True Story of the Three Little Pigs* by Jon Scieszka and Lane Smith (Viking Penguin, 1989).

Prewriting

Explain to students that the prewriting activity will help them think about what they do and do not like in a friend. This will help them plan their response to Ronald. Students can work on prewriting individually or can brainstorm ideas together.

Writing

Remind students that they do not have to include everything from their prewriting lists in their responses to Ronald. They should choose only the best or strongest ideas.

Sharing

When students have finished the writing activity, have volunteers read what they have written and have the class discuss these responses.

Elsa's Pet

Strategy Focus

Using background knowledge to think about a story.

Story at a Glance

A little girl named Elsa learns how to take care of her pet worm by reading about worms with her mother.

Vocabulary

You may want to introduce the following words to your students:

allergic   compost
magnifying   gizzard
bristles

Getting Students Started

• Introducing the Selection

Ask students to talk about their pets, or about pets that belong to their relatives or friends. Discuss what people need to know about an animal in order to keep it as a pet. Explain to students that they are going to read about a little girl who has to learn more about her new pet so that she will know how to take care of it.

• Purpose for Reading

Students read to find out what kind of animal Elsa is going to keep as a pet, and how she learns to take good care of it.

Elsa's Pet

By Maureen Ash

This selection is about a girl named Elsa who wants to have a pet. Read the selection to find out about Elsa's new pet.

"You could get a fish," said Elsa's mother. Elsa knew that her mother was trying to help, but that old answer wasn't any help at all. She was allergic to all the good pets, like cats and dogs.

"The fun part about a pet," Elsa said, "is holding it and petting it. I can't pet a fish."

1 What are some reasons it is fun to have a pet?

14

Possible Responses
Question 1

Holding it and petting it are some reasons it is fun to have a pet.

This student merely repeats what he or she has just read in response to the question. Encourage students to use their own background knowledge to answer the questions.

cute, cuddly, warm, friendly

This student has listed single word ideas. Writing in complete sentences is not necessary for the student to convey ideas and to demonstrate use of background knowledge.

I don't know because I can't have a pet either. They don't let you have pets where I live. I think it would be fun to have a pet, though, because my friend Corrine has a dog named Daisy. Daisy always makes me laugh.

This response indicates that the student is making personal connections to the story in order to facilitate comprehension. Encourage your students to think about personal experiences as they are reading.

"No, not without scaring it," agreed Elsa's mother. "I wish I could help you." She took a bucket from under the sink and wrinkled her nose. "Ick," she said. "Will you take this out to the compost pile, please? It's pretty smelly."

Outside, Elsa dumped the bucket of food scraps onto the compost pile. Something moved on the ground. Elsa squatted down and saw—a worm. It was moving toward a pile of old leaves and grass clippings. As the front end of the worm stretched forward, the worm became long and skinny. Then the worm became shorter and fatter again as it drew its tail end forward.

> 2   What are you thinking about now?

15

Possible Responses
Question 2

I'm thinking that I really don't like worms very much because they're dirty and slimy and they don't smell very good and I don't like them.

This response is a run-on sentence, but the ideas in the sentence indicate that the student is using his or her background knowledge. It is the ideas in the sentence that are important, not the mechanics of the sentence.

If I was Elsa I'd get a dog.

This student has not understood why Elsa cannot get a dog for a pet. The student may not understand the meaning of the word *allergic*. Present the word to students before they begin reading the story by asking if any of them know if they are allergic to anything.

Elsa can't get a dog or a cat. I think she will make the worm her pet.

This student has summarized the main idea of the paragraphs, and then has made a logical prediction about what might happen next.

Encourage students to express their thoughts in writing. For example, in response to the question, "What do you know about worms?" students could draw a picture and write one-word ideas to explain their drawings.

Elsa gently picked up the worm. She held it in front of her face, examining the pink skin and the pattern of rings around its body.

"Hi, worm," Elsa said. "Do you want to be my pet?"

In the house, Elsa placed the worm on a piece of white cardboard. She ran to get her magnifying glass. Peering at her new pet, she saw it raise one end. It seemed to look around.

3 What do you know about worms?

"Do worms have eyes?" Elsa asked.

"No, they don't," answered her mother. "Worms can only feel."

"It has a nose!" exclaimed Elsa. "It has a little nose that sticks out in front."

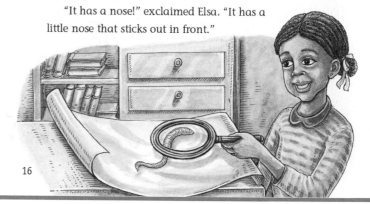

16

Possible Responses
Question 3

Worms live in the mud, are slimy to hold, and are not very smart. I don't think a worm would make a good pet.

This response indicates a good understanding of the story. The student understands that Elsa wants to keep the worm as a pet, and therefore has written what he or she knows about worms in relation to what a worm would be like as a pet.

I don't know why Elsa wants that worm as a pet. I wonder what she'll name it.

Although the student understands the story, he or she has not answered the question. Respond by saying, "That's an interesting response. But what do you know about worms?"

A worm is big and fat. It is usually red or brown. It has rings around its head. I think worms are cool.

This is a good response because the student is expressing an opinion, using background knowledge, and visualizing.

"A nose? I don't think so." Elsa's mother looked through the magnifying glass. "Hmmm," she said. Then she took a book from the shelf. She found a picture and showed it to Elsa.

4   If you wanted to learn more about worms, what would you do?

"That looks like a nose to me, too. But this book says it's a pad of flesh that covers the worm's mouth. When the worm is searching for food, the pad is stretched out. And when it finds food, the pad pulls the food into the worm's mouth and closes over it."

"It's hungry!" exclaimed Elsa. "Let's make a home for it and feed it."

Elsa's mother helped Elsa put some soft dirt into a plastic box for the worm.

Possible Responses
Question 4

Whenever I want to know more about something my mom and me get on the Web.

It is important not to correct students' grammar when they share their responses. This is a good response because the student is showing his or her use of background knowledge and is making connections to personal experiences while reading.

I will read on to find out what happens next.

It is unclear whether this student understands the question. Ask this student to briefly summarize what he or she has just read, and then ask, "Where could you look to learn more about worms?"

I would look up worms in the encyclopedia. I wonder if that's the kind of book Elsa and her mom are using.

This student is not only using his or her background knowledge to facilitate comprehension, but is also questioning the text, which is a good reading strategy.

"What does it eat?" Elsa worried. "I don't want it to starve."

"It won't starve." Elsa's mother brushed dirt from her hands. "Worms eat organic matter."

"Where do we buy that?" Elsa asked.

"Organic matter is stuff that is alive or was alive," Elsa's mother explained. "The potato skins and carrot peelings and dead leaves that we put in the compost pile are all food for worms."

 5 What are you thinking about now?

"Worms eat that stuff?"

"They do," answered Elsa's mother, "after it gets soft from being wet and starts to rot. The worm takes in the organic matter for food. Then the waste comes out the tail end of the worm and makes wonderful fertilizer for our garden. You can even buy it at the garden store—it's called earthworm castings. We'll just mix a few rotten vegetable peelings into this soil, and your worm will have plenty of food."

18

Possible Responses
Question 5

I still don't understand why she wants a worm as a pet. If she's allergic to dogs and cats, why doesn't she get a bird or a turtle? They're not as good as a dog, but they're better than a worm.

This response demonstrates a high level of text comprehension. The student has identified the main ideas of the story and has used that information to question the text. The student has also responded personally to the story.

Is this story trying to get us to want a worm for a pet?

This student is trying to determine one of the author's purposes for writing the story, which is a good response to the text.

I think Elsa is going to keep her worm in the compost pile so that it can eat.

This response indicates that the student is not only using his or her background knowledge to make sense of the text, but is also trying to predict what will happen next in the story.

"Yuk," said Elsa. "It might be better to eat dirt."

6 What do you think about eating dirt?

"Well, worms do eat some dirt. They don't have teeth for chewing, so they need the dirt to help them grind the organic matter into small bits. Then their bodies can absorb it. This grinding happens inside the worm, in its gizzard."

"Birds have gizzards, too," said Elsa.

"That's right," said Elsa's mother.

"And birds eat worms! Our worm is lucky to be away from the robins, right?" asked Elsa.

"Yep, I guess so," her mother answered. "Remember when we saw that robin pulling the worm?"

"Yes," said Elsa. "It was a tug of war."

19

Possible Responses
Question 6

My little sister ate dirt once. She dropped her sucker and it got covered in dirt. She stuck it back in her mouth before my mom could stop her.

This student recalled a personal experience while reading, "'It might be better to eat dirt.'" When this student shares what he or she has written with the class, point out that readers who can relate the story to personal experiences often understand the story better.

I think it's funny that Elsa's mom is helping her with her worm. My mom wouldn't help me take care of a pet that ate dirt. She'd tell me to get rid of it.

This student is carefully thinking about what is happening in the story and is relating it to his or her personal experiences and background knowledge.

I think this is all very gross!

Expressing opinions about what is being read is a legitimate response and should be encouraged.

It is very important to have students discuss what they have written in the boxes to help them focus on what they already know.

Discussing the Think-Alongs

- Give as many students as possible a chance to tell what he or she has written in one of the boxes.
- Have students explain what they were thinking when they wrote.
- Ask students to discuss how their background knowledge helps them think about the story.

Reteaching

For those students who have not written or are having difficulty with the activity:

- Ask them to tell you what they were thinking about as they read.
- Model your own use of background knowledge by sharing the things that you were reminded of as you read the story.
- Ask questions that require students to draw on their background knowledge or personal experiences, such as the following,
- *Did you already know about what worms eat?*
- *Did you already know about the different parts of a worm?*
- *What did you already know about taking care of a pet?*

"Look." Elsa's mother showed Elsa the picture in the book. "See how the worm looks like a lot of rings stuck together? Each of those rings has tiny bristles, called setae. Those bristles are the reason the robin had to pull so hard to get that worm. The setae help the worm hold on tight to the earth when it is partly in its hole. The setae also help the worm crawl forward. And as the worm moves through the soil, it loosens the soil, so air and water can get down to the roots of plants."

"That's another reason we like worms in our garden, right?"

Elsa thought about all the worms she'd seen last summer when they dug up their potatoes.

"You bet," said Elsa's mother. "We like worms."

Elsa petted her worm very gently, placed it in its box, and watched it wriggle its way underground.

7   In what ways would a worm not make a good pet?

20

Possible Responses
Question 7

My cat sits on my lap and keeps me company.

The student needs to elaborate on this response in order to make his or her thoughts more explicit. Ask the student, "I think I understand, but could you tell more about what you're thinking?"

The worm is going to disappear into the dirt. What good is a pet if you never see it?

This response indicates good comprehension of the story. The student has responded to the question by drawing on text he or she has just read, and is also thoughtfully questioning the text.

Do worms live very long? Lots of little animals don't live very long—like only a few weeks or months. We had a fish that died really fast.

This student is using a variety of strategies: background knowledge, making connections to personal experiences, and questioning the text.

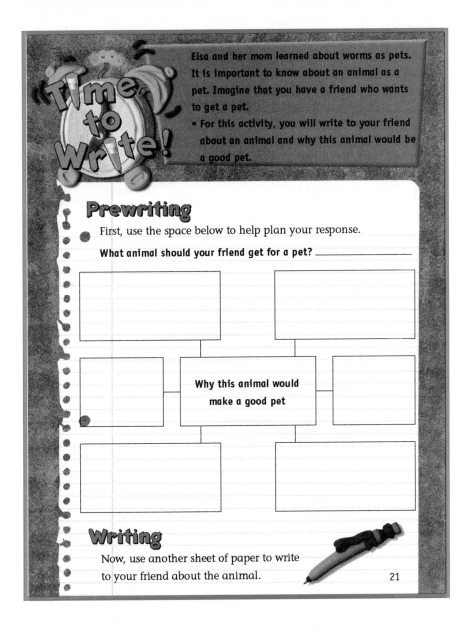

Time to Write!

Elsa and her mom learned about worms as pets. It is important to know about an animal as a pet. Imagine that you have a friend who wants to get a pet.

- For this activity, you will write to your friend about an animal and why this animal would be a good pet.

Prewriting

First, use the space below to help plan your response.

What animal should your friend get for a pet? _____

```
┌─────────────┐                    ┌─────────────┐
│             │                    │             │
│             │                    │             │
│             │                    │             │
└─────────────┘                    └─────────────┘

┌─────────────┐   ┌─────────────────┐   ┌─────────┐
│             │   │  Why this animal │   │         │
│             │   │  would           │   │         │
│             │   │  make a good pet │   │         │
└─────────────┘   └─────────────────┘   └─────────┘

┌─────────────┐                    ┌─────────────┐
│             │                    │             │
│             │                    │             │
│             │                    │             │
└─────────────┘                    └─────────────┘
```

Writing

Now, use another sheet of paper to write to your friend about the animal.

21

Prewriting

Explain to students that the prewriting activity will help them think about all the reasons the animal would make a good pet.

Writing

Remind students that they should give their friend several reasons that the animal they are suggesting would make a good pet.

Sharing

When students have finished the writing activity, make a chart on the chalkboard that illustrates the reasons why students believe different animals would make good pets. On the left side of the chart, vertically list the different pets the students are recommending. On the top of the chart, horizontally list the reasons students give in recommending different animals (cap the list at about six reasons). Encourage students to express various opinions when discussing which reasons go with which animals.

Making Connections

Activity Links

- Have the class watch a documentary about wild animals. Next, organize students into small groups. Ask each group to make two lists: one telling why the animals in the film are interesting or unique, another telling why the animals in the film would not make good pets.
- Have everyone in the class bring in a picture of their pet(s), a picture of a pet belonging to a family member or friend, or pictures of pets from magazines and newspapers. Make a "Pet Collage" with the images to display in the classroom.
- Bring some worms into class and have students look at the worms to see if they can see what Elsa and her mother saw.

Reading Links

You might want to include these books in a discussion of animals that make good pets:

- **The New Puppy** by Laurence Anholt (Artists and Writers Guild, 1995).
- **Enzo the Wonderfish** by Cathy Wilcox (Ticknor & Fields, 1994).
- **My Dog Never Says Please** by Suzanne Williams (Dial Books for Young Readers, 1997).

Strategy Focus

Using background knowledge to think about a story.

Story at a Glance

A boy named Rocco introduces his friends to an unfamiliar food, gnocchi.

Vocabulary

You may want to introduce the following words to your students:

slouched   *sprinkled*
recipe   *kneaded*

Getting Students Started

• Introducing the Selection

Tell students that they are going to read about a boy named Rocco who makes gnocchi. Write the word on the board and pronounce it (NYUH-kee). Have students repeat the pronunciation. Ask them if they know what gnocchi is. Tell them that Rocco teaches his friends how to make gnocchi.

• Purpose for Reading

Students read to find out what gnocchi is.

Rocco's Yucky

By Linda Crotta Brennan

Let's Read

This selection is about a boy named Rocco. He wants to teach his friends how to make gnocchi (NYUH kee). Read the selection to find out what gnocchi is.

Rocco rolled the clay long and thin. Amanda looked at it. "Are you making a snake?" she asked.

"No, I'm making gnocchi," said Rocco.

"What?" asked John, looking up from his clay monster.

"I'm cooking gnocchi," said Rocco. He cut the clay into pieces that looked like little pillows.

"Yucky?" asked Amanda.

"Boys don't cook," said John.

"My father likes to cook," said Rocco. He pushed his thumb into each pillow of clay. "And when we make gnocchi, everybody helps."

 1   What do you think gnocchi might be?

Say NYUH kee.

22

 Possible Responses

Question 1

I think it might be some kind of weird food.

This response indicates that the student is comprehending the story. He or she realizes that gnocchi must be a type of food. Encourage the student to expand upon this response by asking, "What type of food do you think it is?"

I've never heard of gnocchi before.

Some students may feel as though the questions in the boxes have "right answers." If they do not know those answers, they may choose not to attempt an answer. Remind students that there are no wrong answers. Encourage them to write an answer based on what they have read.

Is it clay?

This student has not understood that the students are using the clay to represent other things. Remind students to use their own personal experiences. Ask this student, "What have you made out of clay?"

"Yucky?" said Amanda again.

"Not yucky," said Rocco. "Gnocchi."

John laughed and danced around the classroom. "Yucky, yucky. Rocco cooks yucky!"

When he got home, Rocco slouched in his chair at the kitchen table. "John says boys don't cook."

His father laughed. "How's this for boy cooking?" He gave Rocco a taste of the tomato sauce he was making.

23

Gnocchi

2 cups cold mashed potatoes
2 eggs, slightly beaten
2 cups flour
salt to taste
water as needed
flour as needed

Mix together potatoes, flour, and eggs. Add enough water to make a stiff dough. Knead for five minutes, adding flour if sticky. Roll into snakes. Cut into 1/2- to 1-inch sections. With your thumb, make a dent in the middle of each one. Coat gnocchi with flour and let them dry on a countertop, turning until dry on all sides. Bring a pot of water to a boil and add gnocchi. Cook until they float to the top (about four minutes) and continue cooking for three minutes longer. Serve with tomato sauce, grated cheese, and meat balls or Italian sausage.

Recipe makes 5–6 servings.

"It's good," said Rocco, but he didn't smile. "The kids at school said gnocchi was yucky."

"No one who ever ate gnocchi would think it was yucky," said his father.

That gave Rocco an idea.

"Good thinking," said his father when Rocco told him about it. "I'll call your teacher right now."

 2 What are you thinking about now?

The next morning Rocco carried a big box to school. "Rocco has a surprise for us," his teacher told the class.

Rocco took flour, cold mashed potatoes, eggs, and a bowl out of the box. He propped up a sign with a recipe. On the top it said GNOCCHI: POTATO PASTA.

24

Possible Responses
Question 2

I think that the father will go to school and talk about how he likes to cook.

This is a good prediction because it is well supported by the text. However, it is not what really happens in the story. Point out to students that readers sometimes make predictions that do not happen. They will need to revise predictions as they read.

They will bring some gnocchi to school so that the kids can taste it.

This response demonstrates a good understanding of the story. The student has made a prediction about what might happen next and has supported the prediction with information from the text.

I don't understand why Rocco's friends say that it tastes yucky when they haven't even tried it.

It is possible that this student is not pronouncing the word gnocchi correctly. While not knowing how to pronounce a word when reading silently is usually not important, it is in this story.

Rocco measured the flour into a big bowl.

"Let me break the eggs!" said Amanda.

John added the mashed potatoes. Rocco sprinkled in some water.

Everybody mixed and kneaded the dough. Then they rolled it into wiggly snakes.

"Hey, cooking is fun," John said.

> **3** What do you know about cooking?

They cut the dough into pillows.

"Make a thumbprint in each one," said Rocco.

Then they sprinkled the pillows with flour.

"Now we let them dry overnight," said Rocco.

Amanda rubbed her tummy. "I can't wait."

25

GNOCCHI: POTATO PASTA

Possible Responses
Question 3

. . . .

My mom and I make cookies together. I break the eggs.

Sometimes we make pancakes on the weekend. I know you have to stir.

You have to measure things and read the recipe. My brother and I made a cake for my mom on her birthday.

This question prompts students to make connections to their own personal experiences. Reinforce the importance and appropriateness of this strategy by saying, "I also thought about an experience I had when I was cooking," and then talking about that experience.

It is very important to have the students read and discuss what they have written in the boxes about how they used their background knowledge.

Discussing the Think-Alongs

- Give as many students as possible a chance to tell what they wrote in one of the boxes.
- Have students explain what they were thinking when they wrote.
- Ask students how what they already know helps them think about the story.

Reteaching

For those students who have not written or are having difficulty with the activity:

- Ask students to tell what they were thinking about as they read.
- Model your own use of background knowledge by sharing what the story reminded you of from past experiences.
- Ask questions that require students to draw on their background knowledge or personal experiences, such as the following:
  - *What did you already know about making things with clay?*
  - *What did you already know about cooking?*
  - *What types of things have you shared with your friends before?*

The next day the teacher boiled some water in a big pot. Carefully she put in the gnocchi and let them boil until they floated to the top of the water.

Rocco served the gnocchi with his father's tomato sauce and some cheese.

"Mmm-mm," said the teacher.

John licked his lips. "And I helped cook!"

"This is yummy," said Amanda. "Why do you call it yucky?"

Rocco rolled his eyes. "It's not yucky," he said. "It's gnocchi!"

 4 What are you thinking about now?

26

Possible Responses
Question 4

If I were Rocco I would be getting really tired of people saying "yucky" instead of "gnocchi."

This student recognizes that Rocco's friends have been mispronouncing gnocchi since the beginning of the story. Besides using his or her background knowledge, this student has used the reading strategy of empathizing with a character in the story.

My family makes empañadas. I don't think my friends in my class know what those are. Maybe we can make them in class some day.

This student has thought about how Rocco's family's gnocchi might be like his or her family's empañadas. He or she has thought critically about the story by comparing something in his or her own life to something that has been read.

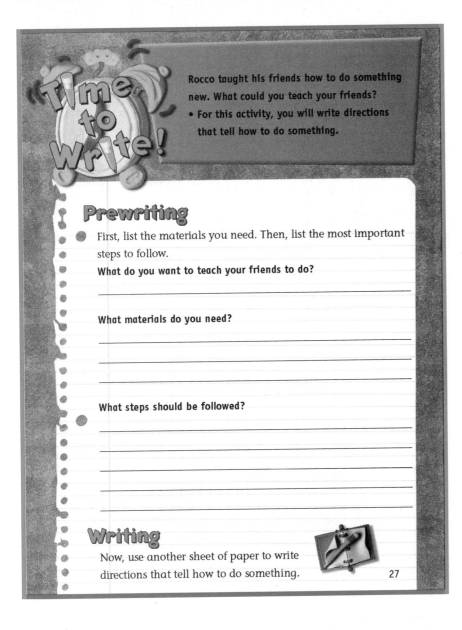

Making Connections

Activity Links

- Have students follow the written directions to complete some of the activities they created for the writing activity.
- Have one or more student volunteers make gnocchi at home with their family. *(See the recipe on page 24 of this guide.)* Ask them to bring some to share with the class.
- Have students explore types of food eaten by people of different cultures around the world. Have students bring in food unique to a particular culture.

Reading Links

You might want to include these books in a discussion of foods that are popular in different cultures:

- **Everybody Cooks Rice** by Norah Dooley (Carolrhoda Books, 1991).
- **The Tortilla Factory** by Gary Paulsen (Harcourt Brace, 1995).
- **A Taste of West Africa** by Colin Harris (Thomson Learning, 1995).

Prewriting

Explain that the prewriting activity will help students organize their thoughts about how they would teach someone to do something. This will help them write directions for their friends.

Writing

Remind students that their directions should be clear enough that someone who has not done the activity before could read their directions to learn how.

Sharing

When students have finished the writing activity, pair students and have them read their directions to each other. Have students provide feedback to each other about whether the directions are clear.

How Things Are Alike and Different

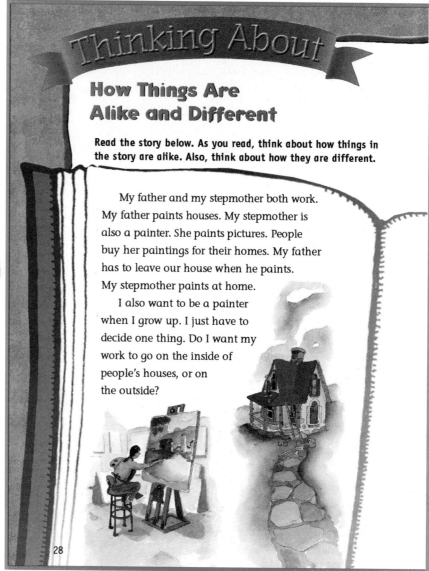

Thinking About

How Things Are Alike and Different

Read the story below. As you read, think about how things in the story are alike. Also, think about how they are different.

My father and my stepmother both work. My father paints houses. My stepmother is also a painter. She paints pictures. People buy her paintings for their homes. My father has to leave our house when he paints. My stepmother paints at home.

I also want to be a painter when I grow up. I just have to decide one thing. Do I want my work to go on the inside of people's houses, or on the outside?

28

Using Comparison and Contrast

Readers frequently compare and contrast characters, events, and settings in stories. Likewise, readers compare and contrast elements of stories to their own lives and surroundings. In science and social studies, comparing and contrasting is a crucial strategy. The activities in this unit will help students to apply the strategy of comparing and contrasting. Therefore, they will better understand and remember what they read.

Introducing the Strategy

Help students identify two characters in stories they have read recently that they think are different from each other. (You may want to suggest one character, and have them think of the second.) Discuss how the characters are different. Then have students think of a third character and discuss how he or she is alike or different from one of the other two. Ask if any of the characters remind them of people they know.

Applying the Strategy

Ask students to follow along as you read the story in the pupil book, or have a volunteer read it. Tell them to think about how things in the story are alike and how they are different.

Did you think of things that are alike and different as you read this story? Answer the questions below.

This story makes me think of different kinds of painting.

How are the father and the stepmother in this story alike?

_____

_____

How are they different?

_____

_____

What else did you think of while you read?

_____

_____

_____

_____

Read and Think

- Read the selections that follow.
- Stop at each box and answer the question.
- Remember to think about how things are alike and different.

29

Read and Think

- Remind students that answering the questions in the boxes will help them think about the selections.
- Tell them that they can write as much or as little as they need to answer the questions.
- Encourage them to think about how things are alike and different as they read the selections.

Discussing the Strategy

Have students complete the questions independently or as a group. Ask students what they were thinking about while the story was read. Have students elaborate on their responses if the connection to the story is not clear.

Ask students to share their responses so they will understand that there are many different ways to make comparisons.

Explain to students that they will use this strategy as they read the selections in this unit.

Strategy Focus

Using comparison and contrast to learn about whales.

Story at a Glance

Whales are mammals that live in the ocean. There are many kinds of whales, many of which have been hunted by people.

Vocabulary

You may want to introduce the following words to your students:

mammal   baleen
harpoon   blubber
blowhole

Getting Students Started

- **Introducing the Selection**

Encourage students to share what they already know about whales. They may know a great deal, but make sure that they understand that the whale is a mammal and is different from a fish. Ask if they know that there are different kinds of whales, and have them suggest how many kinds they think there are.

- **Purpose for Reading**

Students read to learn about whales: how whales are similar to or different from fish, and how whales differ.

Whales: The Gentle Giants

By Joyce Milton

Let's Read. This selection is about whales. Read the selection to learn how whales are alike and different from other animals that live on land and in the sea.

Some whales are as big as small islands. The blue whale is the biggest of all whales. The blue whale is also the biggest animal in the world. A baby blue whale is even bigger than an elephant.

There are about seventy-five different kinds of whales. The sperm whale has a huge head. The male narwhal has one long, twisted tooth. Sometimes this tooth grows to be ten feet long! The pygmy sperm whale is one of the smallest whales. It is about the size of a canoe. That's still pretty big!

1 How are whales different from one another?

30

Possible Responses
Question 1

I didn't know there were so many kinds of whales.

Although this response doesn't answer the question directly, it sets a framework for making comparisons. Respond by asking, "How are some of these whales different from each other?"

I thought all whales were big, but some are biggest of all!

This response reflects an understanding of a significant comparison presented in this section of the text.

They all look different.

Synthesizing details without citing them is a valid reaction. Ask this student, "In what ways do whales look different?"

People used to think that whales were a kind of fish. But a whale is not a fish. It cannot stay underwater all the time. A whale breathes through a hole in its head. This is called a blowhole. When a whale dives, it holds its breath. When it comes up, it breathes out. A big spout of spray comes out of its blowhole. Up it goes, high in the air.

2 How are whales different from fish?

31

Strategy Tip

Suggest to students that when they are reading a selection, a good way to keep track of the details is to sort them into categories for comparison. Remind students that comparing and contrasting is a good way to sort information and understand what is read.

Possible Responses
Question 2

Whales can't stay under all the time.

This student understands an important difference between whales and fish.

Whales have water coming out of their heads.

This student has inferred that "spray" in the text means water, which is a valid reading. However, to be sure that the student understands that whales blow mostly air, not water, from their blow-holes, ask, "What do whales blow from their blowholes?

How do fish and whales breathe differently?"

They both live in water.

This response reaffirms a similarity between fish and whales. To encourage the student to think about how whales and fish are different, say, "Yes, that's true. But how are they different?"

A whale is a mammal. Just like a dog. Just like a cat. Just like you! A baby mammal grows inside its mother's body.

This baby gray whale has just been born. Its mother and another whale quickly push the baby to the top of the water. They are helping the little whale take its first breath of air.

The baby whale is called a calf. It drinks its mother's milk just as a human baby does. It weighs about 2,000 pounds. But to its mother it is still her little baby.

 3   How are whales like land animals?

Usually whales are gentle. But not always. The mother gray whale will fight anything that tries to hurt her calf. The whale calf cannot swim very fast. A big, hungry shark is watching. It is waiting for a chance to attack. But the mother whale is keeping watch too.

32

Possible Responses
Question 3

Whales breathe air.

Whales help their babies.

Focusing on a single supporting detail as a comparison is a legitimate response that suggests that the main idea has been understood. Encourage students to mention other ways that demonstrate that whales are mammals.

Gee! Whales really are like people!

This student's enthusiasm may reflect his or her understanding of the text. To encourage a more direct response to the question, ask the student to describe how whales are like people.

When she sees the shark, she rushes straight at it. Other whales come to help. They swim between the shark and the baby. They are too big for the shark to attack. The shark is not very smart. Soon it is all mixed up. It gives up and swims away. The calf is safe.

4 How are whales smarter than sharks?

33

Possible Responses
Question 4

Sharks are dumb.
This response reflects an understanding of details from the passage. Encourage the student to think about how whales are smarter by asking, "What did the whales do to chase the shark away?"

The shark got mixed up.
This response indicates an understanding of the text and an implicit comparison. To clarify this comparison, ask the student to describe what the whales did to confuse the shark.

Maybe the shark will come back.
This is a thoughtful prediction.

All winter long the baby gray whale swims and plays in the warm waters off the coast of Mexico. But when spring comes, the gray whales are on the move. They will swim all the way to cold Arctic waters. Even the baby whale will make the long trip.

They swim day and night. But sometimes even a whale gets tired. When the whales are sleepy, they lie on top of the water and take naps.

> **5** How do whales sleep differently from how you sleep?

34

Possible Responses
Question 5

They sleep right in the water. I would sink. Why don't they sink?

This is a strong response because the student relies on his or her background knowledge and personal experience to make a thoughtful comment about whales. During discussion have this student ask other students why they think whales don't sink.

I like to sleep in a bed with my favorite pillow.

This student understands the question, but it isn't clear how much of the story he or she understands. Encourage the student to use information from the text to make a comparison by asking, "How do whales like to sleep?"

If they sleep sometimes, they don't swim every day and night, do they?

Challenging the logic and consistency of a text indicates careful thinking that relies on a close reading of the text.

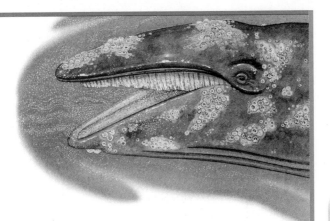

After their long trip the gray whales are very hungry. The cold water is filled with their favorite food—tiny sea animals, so small you would not think they could feed a whale. But they do. The whales open their mouths wide. SLURP! They take in lots of water. And *lots* of tiny sea animals too.

Like many whales, the gray whale has no teeth. Instead it has baleen. The baleen grows in long strips. It works like a big strainer. When a whale spits out a mouthful of water, lots of the tiny sea animals stay caught in its baleen. They will be the whale's dinner.

People did not always know that whales make sounds. Sailors in submarines used to hear strange things: CLICKETY-CLICK! CRRRACK! The noises sounded like music from outer space. The sailors were surprised to learn that all those sounds were made by whales.

35

Meeting Individual Needs

Have volunteers pretend to be an adult whale and a baby whale, swimming along the U.S. coast. They see boats with people. Have students make up conversations between the whales that rely on facts they learned from the passage or on things they already know.

Humpback whales make the strangest sounds of all. They seem to be singing. Humpbacks are funny looking. Their heads are covered with bumps. But the songs they sing are beautiful. Scientists have even recorded the songs of the humpbacks. What do the songs mean? So far scientists are not sure.

6 What have people learned about whales?

Possible Responses
Question 6

They made all kinds of sounds.

This is a good summary of some of the text presented in this section.

How do whales make the noise? What are the whales doing?

This is a very good question that would make a good focus for class discussion. The implication in the selection is that the whales are "singing," but it doesn't really say this. Some students may want to research this question.

How did the sailors hear the whales? Why would being in a sub help?

This is a very good response because the student uses background knowledge and logically challenges the text. Ask the student to share these interesting questions during discussion.

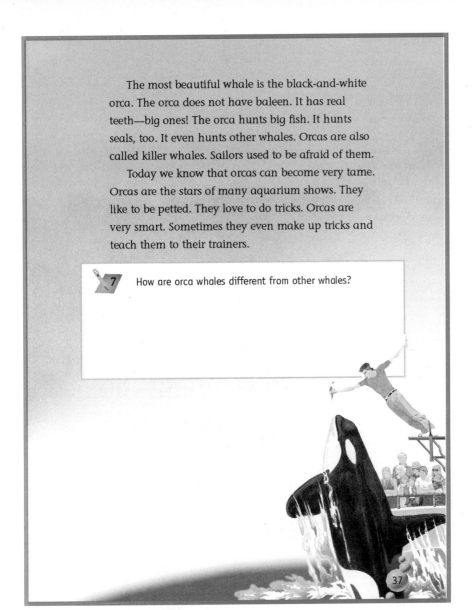

The most beautiful whale is the black-and-white orca. The orca does not have baleen. It has real teeth—big ones! The orca hunts big fish. It hunts seals, too. It even hunts other whales. Orcas are also called killer whales. Sailors used to be afraid of them.

Today we know that orcas can become very tame. Orcas are the stars of many aquarium shows. They like to be petted. They love to do tricks. Orcas are very smart. Sometimes they even make up tricks and teach them to their trainers.

7 How are orca whales different from other whales?

37

Possible Responses
Question 7

Orcas have teeth and eat other things with them.

This is a very good response in which the student has chosen details from the text to support an answer. Encourage the student to make the comparison between orcas and other whales more explicit by asking, "How do other whales eat if they don't have teeth?"

Orcas like to do tricks.

This is a good response that implies a comparison with other whales. Ask the student, "Do you think other whales would do tricks?"

The sailors didn't need to be afraid of the killer whales. It is not a fair name! We kill them, they don't kill us!

This sensitive response reflects a good understanding of the text and the history of the relationship between whales and people. To encourage this student to answer the question, respond by saying, "That is a very good point. Now can you tell how orca whales are different from other whales?"

Orcas do not hunt people. But for many years people hunted whales. Why? Mostly they wanted the whales' blubber. Blubber is a kind of thick fat. It can be made into oil. Years ago whale oil was burned in lamps. That's how people lit their houses.

Ships spent many months at sea looking for whales. The hunters searched for whales in the cold seas of the far north. Sometimes the ships got stuck in the ice. Some never returned.

Hunting whales was dangerous work. When they found a whale, the hunters chased it in small boats. They threw long spears called harpoons into the whale's back. The whale fought hard to get away. A frightened whale could overturn a boat!

So many whales were killed that few were left. People started to worry about saving the whales. Laws were passed to protect whales. Today most people who follow whales only want to watch them.

8 Why do people today not need whale oil?

39

Possible Responses
Question 8

Because they don't use oil lamps.

This is a reasonable response in which the student uses background knowledge to illustrate a cause-and-effect relationship. Encourage the student to think about what has replaced oil lamps by asking, "What do people use instead of oil lamps?"

We light our houses with light-bulbs now.

This student has thoughtfully used background knowledge to explain the cause-and-effect relationship indicated by the question.

Because so many whales were killed.

This response reflects information presented in this section of text, but does not accurately address the question. Ask the student to reread the passage that explains how people used blubber for oil. Then ask, "What do people use now instead of oil lamps?"

To help students focus on similarities and differences, have them read and discuss what they have written in the boxes.

Discussing the Think-Alongs

- Encourage each student to share what he or she has written in one of the boxes.
- Have students explain what they were thinking as they wrote their responses.
- Have students discuss similarities and differences among several kinds of whales.

Reteaching

For those students who have not written or are having difficulty with the activity:

- Read aloud the first section of the article and model your own use of comparing and contrasting by discussing your thoughts as you read.
- Encourage students to think about how their background knowledge helps them compare and contrast information in the selection. Talk to students about what they knew about whales before they began reading. How did the article change what they knew about whales?
- Motivate the students to compare and contrast by asking:
  - *How are whales the same as fish?*
  - *How are they different from fish?*
  - *How are different kinds of whales different from each other?*

Scientists watch whales to learn about their lives in the sea. Whale watching is also fun. Whales seem to like watching people, too. They will swim and play around a boat for a long time. If you go whale watching, you might even see a whale jump high in the air. Why do whales jump? No one knows. Maybe they jump just because it feels so good to be a whale!

 9 How do people treat whales differently today than they did many years ago?

40

Possible Responses
Question 9

Now they say "Save the whales!"
This student has combined a synthesis of the text with his or her background knowledge. In discussion, ask the student to clarify how people treated whales before they wanted to save them. Have the class discuss how people try to protect whales today.

People watch them and don't kill them.
This is a very good response because it refers to two primary points in the text. In discussion, encourage this

student to remember more details from the selection about why people killed whales, and why people watch them today.

Whales seem to like people now.
This student has used information from the text to implicitly compare how whales viewed people today and in the past. However, the student has not answered the question. Ask, "How do people treat whales differently than they did in the past?"

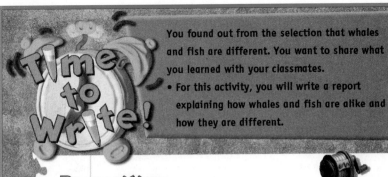

You found out from the selection that whales and fish are different. You want to share what you learned with your classmates.
• For this activity, you will write a report explaining how whales and fish are alike and how they are different.

Prewriting

First, use this chart to show how whales and fish are alike and how they are different. The first two facts are done for you.

Characteristic	Whales	Fish
They live in water.	yes	yes
They come to the surface to breathe.	yes	no
Their babies are born alive.		
They drink their mother's milk.		
They are hatched from eggs.		
They are very good swimmers.		
They hold their breath underwater.		
They stay underwater all the time.		

Writing

Now, use another sheet of paper to write your report about how whales and fish are alike and different.

41

Making Connections

Activity Links

- Have students make posters featuring different kinds of whales and ask them to create a display or present their artwork to the class.
- Ask students to use the Internet to research how people hunted and killed whales in the past, and how people are trying to protect whales today.
- Have students create a chart to compare and contrast different types of whales, or to compare whales to other mammals, such as dogs or cats.

Reading Links

You may want to include these books in a discussion on whales:
- **The Atlantic Gray Whale (Gone Forever)** by Jan Mell (Crestwood House, 1989).
- **Captain Jim and the Killer Whales** by Carol Amato (Barron Juveniles, 1995).
- **Bees Dance and Whales Sing: The Mysteries of Animal Communication** by Margery Facklam (Sierra Club Juveniles, 1992).

Prewriting

Explain to students that the prewriting activity will help them more clearly understand the differences and similarities between whales and fish.

Writing

Encourage students to write their reports with the idea that the person who is reading it knows very little about whales. Tell students to write clearly and use examples that will help someone picture how whales look and act.

Sharing

Organize students into small groups and have them present their reports to each other. Encourage students to point out what they think is really clear in their classmates' reports and ask them to explain what could be clearer. You may want to invite a group of students into the class who have not read the whales article and have some of your students present their reports to the visiting students.

Diego Rivera: An Artist's Life

Diego Rivera: An Artist's Life

By Sarah Vázquez

Strategy Focus

Using comparison and contrast to learn about Diego Rivera.

Story at a Glance

Diego Rivera was a Mexican artist who became famous for his paintings and murals.

Vocabulary

You may want to introduce the following words to your students:

murals	styles
mosaic	self-portraits

Getting Students Started

· Introducing the Selection

Ask students to suggest several kinds of art forms with which they are familiar, and write these on the chalkboard. Call on students to identify which of these art forms they most like to look at or create, and ask them to discuss why. Tell students that they are going to read a story about a Mexican artist named Diego Rivera, who worked with a variety of art forms.

· Purpose for Reading

Students read to find out about all the styles that Diego Rivera used in creating his artwork.

Let's Read

Diego Rivera was a famous Mexican artist. During his life, he tried many different painting styles. Read the selection to find out about the different painting styles he used.

Diego Rivera was born in 1886 in a town called Guanajuato. It is high in the mountains of Mexico. Diego had a twin brother named Carlos. His parents were very happy when the twins were born. Their other babies had died.

42

Diego Rivera was named after his father. His father worked as a teacher. He also visited other schools to make sure they were teaching the children well. Diego's parents helped poor people. His parents wanted everyone to have a better life.

 1 How are Diego's parents like someone you know?

Diego loved toy trains. One of his favorite things to do was to take them apart. He wanted to see how trains worked.

Diego also loved to draw. He began drawing when he was just three. He liked to draw trains. He drew everywhere he could reach. He drew on the chairs, on the walls, on the floor, or on paper.

 43

 Strategy Tip

Ask students to think about how their own interests and abilities in art, music, or dance compare with Diego Rivera's artistic talents and interests. Discuss the use of comparing and contrasting in helping students to better understand the story.

Possible Responses
Question 1

They are very nice like my grandma and grandpa. My grandma and grandpa always do things for me like help me with my homework.
This student is not only comparing Diego's parents to his or her grandparents, but is also relating the story to personal experiences.

This is like people who give money and clothes to the poor.
This student has not mentioned a specific person he or she knows, but the response does demonstrate an understanding of what is being read.

Diego's parents are nice people because they help others.
This student has summarized the main point of this paragraph, but has not made a clear comparison. You might ask the student, "Who is someone you know who helps other people? How is this person like Diego's parents?"

Diego spent much of his time drawing.
Sometimes he drew on the walls of his bedroom.
His parents didn't want him to draw there, so they
covered the walls in his room with plain paper. Then
Diego was free to draw on his walls. That is how he
painted his first wall paintings. These wall paintings
are called murals.

 2 How might painting a mural be more difficult than painting a picture on paper?

 Possible Responses
Question 2

My mom would never cover my walls in paper so I could draw on them.

Although this student is not responding directly to the question, he or she is comparing his or her mother to Diego's mother. Ask, "How would painting a mural be different from painting a picture on paper?"

You would need more ideas.

This response is thoughtful, but needs to be expanded. When students are sharing their responses, ask this student to explain what he or she was thinking.

I don't think you could paint a mural sitting down.

This response reflects a very good understanding of the difference between painting a mural and painting a picture. This student is probably applying the strategy of visualization as well as comparing and contrasting.

Diego the Student

When Diego was ten years old, he started using paints to add colors to his drawings. Then he decided to be a painter. His parents let him take art classes after school.

After high school, young Diego went to the San Carlos School of Fine Arts. There he learned to love the art of the Mexican Indians. Their art showed the land, people at work, and their animals.

Diego learned many lessons from his teacher. Diego's teacher had a shop in Mexico City. He drew cartoons that made people laugh. He liked to draw poor people as being very good and rich people as being bad.

Diego began to paint this way, too. In 1906, some of his paintings were in an art show. He began to sell his paintings to earn money. His paintings sold well.

 3   What are you thinking about now?

45

Possible Responses
Question 3

How did Diego get his painting into an art show?

This response shows that the student understands one of the main points in the preceding paragraph.

I'm thinking about whether or not Diego Rivera's twin brother was also good at painting, and if they will talk about him again in the story.

This response reveals that the student is thinking about information presented earlier to make predictions about what he or she might read later in the text.

I would like to see what Diego has painted because I think I would like it.

This response indicates excellent comprehension of the text. The student clearly understands what he or she is reading, and even provides a personal reaction to the text.

Diego the Painter

Diego Rivera wanted to learn more about painting. He went to Europe in 1907 to study. He tried many different painting styles. He liked paintings that showed real people in real places. He did not like the modern styles where things did not look real.

In 1921, Diego went back to Mexico. He painted a mural for a school. He showed many Indian people in this mural. He painted with bright, strong colors. The shapes were large and simple. This was his own style.

Diego also used many pieces of colored glass to make murals. They are called mosaic murals.

His Marriage

In 1928, Diego met an artist named Frida Kahlo. She was in art school, and Diego was painting a mural there. She went to see him about her paintings. They became friends and got married a year later. In the following years, they became famous together.

 4 How did Diego's life and art change?

Frida had been in pain much of her life. Frida had polio as a child and was in a bus wreck in her teens. While she was ill, she taught herself to paint. She painted many self-portraits.

 47

Possible Responses
Question 4

It was better.
This response needs to be expanded. It is a good response if the student can support the statement with information from the text. However, if the student is unable to explain his or her answer, ask, "How did Diego's life change for the better? How did his art change for the better?"

He made mosaic murals.
This student has chosen a discrete piece of information to respond to the question. The student has used the strategy of rereading to find an appropriate response. To encourage the student to clarify the comparison, ask, "What did he make before he made mosaic murals?"

Diego Rivera got married.
It is not unusual for a student to respond to a question using the most recent information he or she has read. Encourage this student to respond to the other part of the question by asking, "How did Diego's art change after he returned to Mexico?"

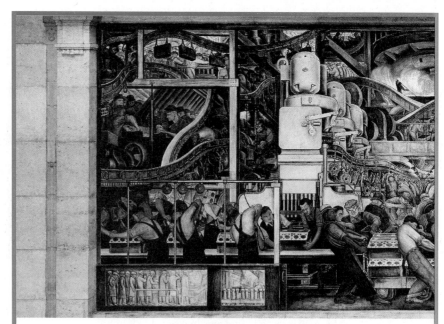

His Later Years

In 1931, there was an art show in New York City with 150 of Diego's paintings. Many other artists came to study with him. He became famous for his style of painting murals. He liked painting pictures that could be seen by many people in public places.

In 1932, the City of Detroit hired Diego for a huge job. He painted 27 murals on four walls of the Detroit Institute of Arts.

48

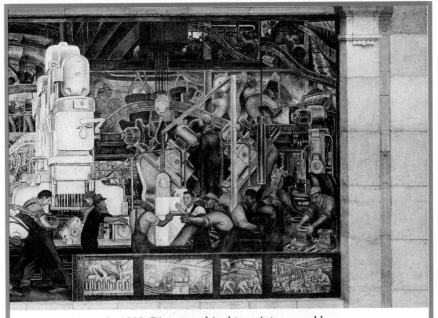

In 1933, Diego was hired to paint a mural by a man in New York City. But when the man saw the people in the mural, he did not like one person shown. He asked Diego to change it, but Diego would not. After Diego was paid, the man had the mural painted over. Later, Diego painted a smaller mural of this scene in Mexico City.

> **5** What are you thinking about now?
>
> 49

Possible Responses
Question 5

I would be mad if I was Diego Rivera. That man had seen Diego's murals before, and he shouldn't have hired him if he didn't like them.

This student's response indicates an excellent understanding of what has just been read. The student has evaluated what has been read and expressed an opinion based on that evaluation.

Rivera was a very talented artist. He seemed to like to paint in Mexico more than anywhere else.

In the second part of this response, the student has drawn a conclusion based on what he or she has read.

This makes me think about how much I like to paint. I have always liked to paint from the time I was little. Maybe I'll be a famous artist like Diego Rivera. I don't think I want to paint murals, though.

This student is not only using the strategy of comparing and contrasting, but is also relating personal experiences to what is being read.

To help students focus on how things are alike and different, have them read and discuss what they have written in the boxes.

Discussing the Think-Alongs

- Give as many students as possible a chance to tell what they have written in one of the boxes.
- Have students explain what they were thinking when they wrote their responses.
- Ask students how thinking about similarities and differences helped them think about the story.

Reteaching

For those students who have not written or are having difficulty with the activity:

- Ask them to discuss what they were thinking about as they read.
- Model your own use of comparison and contrast by sharing what you compared as you read.
- Ask questions about how things in the story are alike and how they are different:
- *How is painting a mural different from painting on a piece of paper?*
- *In what ways were Diego Rivera and his wife alike?*
- *How were Diego Rivera's experiences in Mexico different from his experiences in the United States?*

After that, Diego had hard times for a while. He lost some jobs in the United States. He didn't sell as much there. But he kept busy painting in Mexico.

In 1950, Diego Rivera won Mexico's National Art Prize. His country held a big party for him on his seventieth birthday. But in 1955, he became ill, and he died a year later.

Diego Rivera's art lives on. Many of his paintings and murals are in museums all around the world. Some of his best murals can be seen in the National Palace in Mexico City. Because of his beautiful artwork, people will always remember Diego Rivera.

50

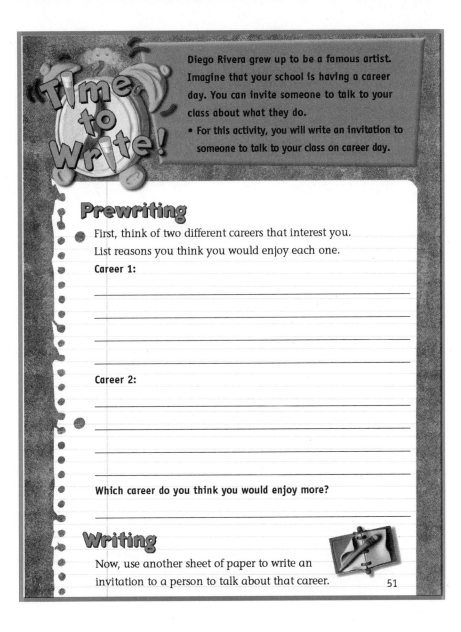

Diego Rivera grew up to be a famous artist. Imagine that your school is having a career day. You can invite someone to talk to your class about what they do.

• For this activity, you will write an invitation to someone to talk to your class on career day.

Prewriting

First, think of two different careers that interest you. List reasons you think you would enjoy each one.

Career 1:

_____

_____

_____

_____

Career 2:

_____

_____

_____

_____

Which career do you think you would enjoy more?

_____

Writing

Now, use another sheet of paper to write an invitation to a person to talk about that career.

51

Making Connections

Activity Links

- Ask students to help organize a career day. Have them send the invitations that they wrote. Encourage each student to make a list of questions he or she can ask class visitors.
- Have students access the World Wide Web or go to the library to find images of murals and other works by Diego Rivera.
- Have the class paint a large mural on either a wall of the school or on a large piece of butcher paper taped to the wall of the classroom. Before students begin painting, discuss a theme for their artwork.

Reading Links

You might want to include these books in a discussion of art, artists, or careers:

- **The Art Lesson** by Tomie dePaolo (The Trumpet Club, 1989).
- **Introducing Rembrandt** by Alexander Sturgis (Little, Brown, 1994).
- **Painting: A Young Artist's Guide** by Elizabeth Waters and Annie Harris (Dorling Kindersley, 1993).
- **Chicken Soup, Boots** by Maira Kalman (Viking, 1993).

Prewriting

Explain to students that the prewriting activity will help them think about different careers. Ask students to write about what they might want to be when they grow up. Students can work on the prewriting activity individually, or they can brainstorm ideas together.

Writing

Remind students to use the parts of a letter when they write the invitation. Tell them to include why this career interests them.

Sharing

When students have finished the writing activity, organize them into pairs and have the members of each pair read their thoughts about future careers to each another. Next, ask each pair to make a list of how the careers they wrote about are alike or different.

A Look at Spiders

A Look at Spiders
By Jerald Halpern

Strategy Focus

Using comparison and contrast to learn about many kinds of spiders.

Story at a Glance

This article presents many facts about spiders. It discusses their body parts, emphasizes how they vary in size, describes what spiders eat and where they live, and tells whether spiders are dangerous to people.

Vocabulary

You may want to introduce the following words to your students:

pinchers	spinners
zigzag	prey
keen	

Getting Students Started

- **Introducing the Selection**

  Ask students to share what they know about spiders and how they feel about them. Ask if students think spiders are insects. Ask if they know what spiders eat, where they live, and how they make webs. Tell them they will be reading about different kinds of spiders and about the different parts of a spider's body.

- **Purpose for Reading**

  Students read to learn new information about spiders by contrasting spiders and insects, and by comparing and contrasting different types of spiders.

Let's Read

This selection is about spiders. Read the selection to find out about different kinds of spiders. Also, find out how spiders are different from insects.

What Is a Spider?

Some people think that spiders are insects, but they are not. Both spiders and insects have a hard covering on the outside of their bodies. Spiders have eight legs and no wings. Insects have six legs and usually do have wings.

1   How are spiders different from insects?

52

Possible Responses
Question 1

It's got eight legs, not six, and no wings!

This student has understood both major distinguishing factors of spiders in the first paragraph.

Don't ask me to touch it!

Spiders are apt to generate strong personal reactions from some students. You might want to emphasize the potential to compare and contrast here by asking, "How could you tell a spider from an insect without touching it?"

I always thought spiders were insects.

This is a thoughtful response that shows the student is reading closely and critically, and is also using background knowledge.

All spiders have the same body parts. The main part of their body is divided into two sections. In the front, there are eight legs and two pinchers. Special parts in the back, called spinnerets, make silk. Spiders use the silk to make webs.

Spiders have five senses. Their sense of touch is the strongest. They can feel anything that moves near them. They use their mouth and front pinchers to taste and smell food. To see, most spiders have eight eyes. Spiders have small openings on their legs to help them hear sounds.

 2 What are you thinking about now?

Strategy Tip

Remind students that one way to learn about spiders is to think about how various types of spiders can be alike and different. One spider, for example, may be much smaller or bigger than another. However, all spiders have the same kinds of body parts. Comparing and contrasting is a good way for students to learn and remember what they read.

Possible Responses
Question 2

They have lots of eyes. It would be neat to have eight eyes!

This student has focused on one of the many details in this section of the text. To encourage the student to compare and contrast, ask, "What other animals have more than two eyes?"

Ears on their legs? That's a funny place to have ears.

This student has chosen to discuss an interesting detail, which shows that he or she is thinking critically about the text.

I saw a spider move fast when there was a fly caught in its web.

This student has not responded directly to the question or demonstrated that he or she understands the details in this section. However, the student is relating the topic to a personal experience.
To refocus the student on comparing and contrasting, ask, "Can you think of any ways that spiders and flies are different?"

How Big Are Spiders?

Spiders can be very large. They can even grow bigger than an adult's hand. But spiders can also be much smaller. Some never get bigger than the top of a pin. Female spiders are always larger than male spiders.

Tarantulas are the largest spiders in the world. Those found in South America can be as long as a sheet of paper. Comb-footed spiders are the smallest spiders. They can be as small as the point of a pencil.

 3 How do spiders compare in size?

Possible Responses
Question 3

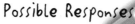

Some spiders are so small you can't even see them.

This response reflects an accurate interpretation of the text. Ask the student, "What object did the author compare the size of the smallest spider to?" or "How big is the largest spider?"

Yiiiike! I would hate to see a tarantula!

This student offers a personal reaction to the reading. To encourage the student to compare and contrast different spiders, ask "How are tarantulas different from other spiders? How are they similar?"

I wonder why female spiders are bigger.

This is a thoughtful response that shows strong critical thinking skills. Encourage this student to find the answer to his or her question in the library or on the Internet.

Where Do Spiders Live?

Spiders live in many places. They live at the top of mountains or on the bottom of caves. Some live in damp areas. Others live in deserts. Some spiders live on the ground, some in trees, and some in buildings.

The water spider lives in a pond. It makes a silk home on underwater plants. The spider traps a bubble of air and brings it below to its home. This is how the spider can breathe while in the water.

Most spiders live in silk webs they have built. Some webs have a round shape. Some webs have a zigzag look, and some look like tents. A spider's web is amazing to see.

4   What are different places spiders live?

55

★ ESOL

Ask students who can read and speak a second language to share with the class what people in other countries think about spiders. Have students discuss the following questions:
- What spiders live in other countries that don't live in the U.S.?
- What are the names for the different spiders that live in these other places?

Possible Responses
Question 4

Spiders can live anywhere.
This is a logical assumption given the information presented in the selection, but it probably is not accurate. Encourage the student to distinguish between different types of spiders by asking, "Would the spider who lives in the desert be able to live in water?"

Some spiders live in mountains and other spiders live in deserts.
This is an accurate summary that shows a good understanding of the text.

There are lots of spiders in my garage at home.
Relating what is being read to personal experience is always a good response. Encourage this student to think about the different places that spiders can live by saying, "Yes, spiders often live in buildings. Where else can spiders live?"

How Do Spiders Make Silk?

Spiders make silk inside their bodies. It is squeezed out like toothpaste through the spinnerets. The silk is like thread that gets hard. Spiders use their silk in different ways.

Most spiders use their silk to weave a web. But not all spiders make webs. Some use silk to make a bed on a leaf. Others use silk to line tunnels in the ground. Many spiders use silk to wrap up insects so they can eat them later.

 5 What different ways do spiders use silk?

56

Possible Responses
Question 5

Not all spiders make webs, but they all make silk.

This response offers a nice synthesis of the main point by relying on comparison and contrast. To encourage this student to more directly answer the question, ask, "What do the spiders that do not make webs do with the silk they make?"

They make beds.

This is a brief response that focuses on one detail from the text. Encourage the student to compare this type of spider with others by asking, "What do other spiders do with their silk?"

Different spiders use their silk for different stuff.

Because this student has restated the question, it is unclear whether he or she understands the details presented in the text. Ask the student to summarize some of the points from the preceding passage, focusing on comparing and contrasting spiders' different uses of silk.

How Do Spiders Eat?

Spiders have a strange way of eating. They turn their food into a liquid. Then they drink the liquid. It is like drinking milk through a straw!

Spiders are picky eaters. They usually eat only insects. Sometimes they may eat small frogs or lizards. First they trap the prey in their web. Then they poison it with a bite.

6 What interested you about the way spiders eat?

Possible Responses
Question 6

How could a spider eat a frog!
   Critically questioning the text is a good reading strategy, but it is not clear whether this student has understood how spiders eat their prey. Encourage this student to reread the first paragraph and think about ways spiders might turn frogs into a liquid meal.

I knew they were all poisonous, but I didn't know that's how they ate.
   The text has reinforced this student's background knowledge and has led to a deeper

understanding of the topic. Ask, "Why do you think spiders need to be poisonous to eat their food?"

How do they do that? Turn their victims into liquid and then drink them? Ugh!!!!
   This is a good question that reflects strong critical thinking skills. Encourage this student to look for an answer to his or her question in the library or on the Internet.

What Kinds of Spiders Are There?

There are many different kinds of spiders. Spiders can be different in color and in size. They can also be different in the ways they move and how they hunt for their prey.

Tarantulas are very large and hairy. They are the biggest of all the spiders. Tarantulas use sharp fangs to bite and kill their prey. They can also shed their long hairs to poison their prey.

Jumping spiders have short legs, but they are able to jump very far. Two of their legs are used just for jumping. These spiders jump to sneak up on insects. They jump again to catch them.

Trap-door spiders dig tunnels in the ground. They line the tunnels with silk they have spun. Then the spiders make a door made of silk and dirt. Trap-door spiders spend the day inside with the door closed. At night, they raise the door and go out to trap insects.

 7 What are you thinking about now?

58

Possible Responses
Question 7

I didn't know there were so many kinds to know about.

This is a reasonable response that summarizes the main point of the section.

How can a spider make a trap door?

This student either disbelieves that spiders can make trap doors, or is interested in learning how spiders go about making them. Ask this student to clarify his or her response, and encourage him or her to further explore how spiders make trap doors.

I hate hairy spiders. They look bad.

This is a strong personal reaction, which is a valid response to the text. In discussion, encourage this student to talk about the ways that even hairy spiders might be interesting.

A wolf spider is a very good hunter. It has keen eyesight and is able to move quickly. During the day, the wolf spider searches for insects. When it sees one, it races up and catches it.

Crab spiders move sideways slowly, just like crabs do. Crab spiders often trap and eat bees and butterflies. Sometimes they can change their body color to match what is around them. This helps them catch their food.

> **8** What different ways do spiders catch their food?

Possible Responses
Question 8

Spiders are always killing other insects. They seem mean to me.

This is a personal reaction to the eating habits of spiders. To encourage this student to respond to the question, ask, "What are some of the ways that different spiders catch their food?"

I think we had a wolf spider in our house. My dad killed it. It seemed to just kind of crumble up.

This student is clearly interested in the text, but has not addressed the question. To redirect the student, ask, "How is the wolf spider different from the crab spider?"

Speed and special tricks help them catch stuff! They also can make traps.

This response reflects good comprehension of the text. Respond by asking, "What are some of the different tricks that spiders use to catch their prey? Can you name any of the spiders that use these different tricks?"

It is important to have students discuss what they have written in the boxes about comparing and contrasting.

Discussing the Think-Alongs

- Give as many students as possible a chance to tell what they wrote as one of their responses.
- Discuss with students how they used the strategy of comparison and contrast. Ask questions such as the following:
  - *How are insects different from spiders?*
  - *Do you think all spiders have the same body parts?*
- Encourage students to explain the connections between what they have written and what they have read, whether or not their responses use comparison and contrast.

Reteaching

For those students who have not written or are having difficulty with the activity:

- Ask them to tell what they were thinking about as they read.
- Read the first part of the article aloud and model your own use of comparing and contrasting as you read.
- Suggest that students keep additional notes as they read. Have them make a chart comparing and contrasting insects and spiders, or have them draw pictures that show the similarities and differences between insects and spiders.

Can Spiders Harm People?

Few spiders are harmful to people. All spiders use their poison when they bite their prey. But their poison rarely harms people. Usually a spider bite just itches.

In North America, there are only six kinds of spiders that can harm people. The most dangerous is the black widow. This spider's poison is stronger than a rattlesnake's. The female black widow spider is the one that bites.

 9 What are you thinking about now?

If you find a spider, look at it carefully. Count its legs. See its colors. Notice its beautiful web. Spiders are very interesting to watch!

60

Possible Responses
Question 9

There's lots of new stuff about spiders in here. It won't make me like them, though.
This student is reacting to the new information in the text with a personal opinion, which is a valid response.

Does the spider die after she bites a person? I heard she does.
This response uses background knowledge to go beyond the text, which reflects strong critical thinking skills. Encourage this student to find the answer to his or her question by looking in the library or on the Internet.

Hey, I want to know what the other five kinds are. What do they look like? I want to know! Why doesn't this tell me?
Challenging the text and hoping for more information reflects active engagement with the text. Encourage this student to look in other sources for additional information about spiders.

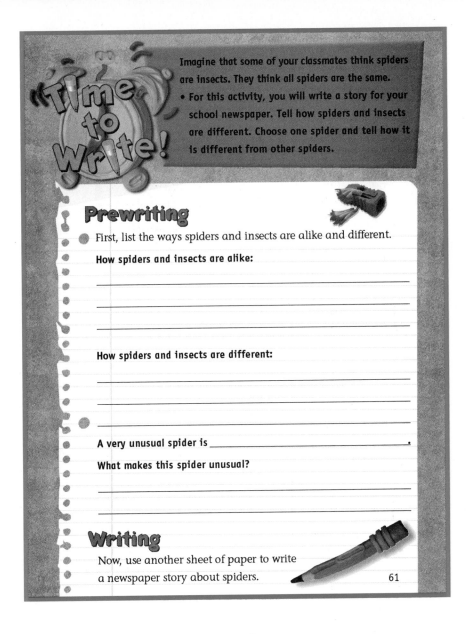

Making Connections

Activity Links

- Have students prepare a report on spider webs or different types of spiders using library and Internet resources. They may also wish to include information about other forms of life that prepare and use traps. Have students work individually or in small groups.
- Find the traditional poem "Miss Muffet" and encourage students to discuss different ways that people react to spiders.
- Encourage students to write and perform a play with spiders as characters. Have them make their own web as a set.

Reading Links

You might want to include the following books in a discussion about spiders:

- **Charlotte's Web** by E. B. White (Harper Trophy, 1974).
- **Extremely Weird Spiders** by Sarah Lovett (John Muir Publications, 1996).
- **Adios, Chi Chi: The Adventures of a Tarantula** by Carol A. Amato and Nicole Amato (Barrons Juveniles, 1996).

Within the image:

Time to Write!

Imagine that some of your classmates think spiders are insects. They think all spiders are the same.
- For this activity, you will write a story for your school newspaper. Tell how spiders and insects are different. Choose one spider and tell how it is different from other spiders.

Prewriting

First, list the ways spiders and insects are alike and different.

How spiders and insects are alike:

_____

_____

_____

How spiders and insects are different:

_____

_____

_____

A very unusual spider is _____.

What makes this spider unusual?

_____

_____

Writing

Now, use another sheet of paper to write a newspaper story about spiders.

61

Prewriting

Explain that the prewriting activity will help students organize their thoughts before writing a newspaper story.

Writing

Remind students to write their stories for people who do not know the differences between insects and spiders. Tell them to ask themselves questions such as the following:

- *Will the reader know how spiders and insects are different?*
- *Will the reader understand why the spider I described is unusual?*

Sharing

Organize students into small groups. Have them take turns acting as "editors" and "reporters." As one student (the "reporter") reads his or her story, the other group members (the "editors") point out parts of the story that are unclear. Encourage them to also point out clearly written sections in each story.

Thinking Along on Tests

The Tests

The next three selections are like standardized-test reading comprehension passages, with questions at the end of each selection. However, boxes with think-along questions appear within the selections to allow students to practice their think-along strategies.

Note that these selections are not designed to test specific reading strategies, but rather are designed to show students how thinking along will help them comprehend what they are read-ing and better answer questions about what they have read.

Introducing the Tests to Students

Ask students to share their ideas about test taking, such as how they go about answer-ing multiple-choice questions. They may say that they read the selection and then answer the questions at the end. Tell them that for these selections, they will apply the think-along process, stopping at cer-tain places in the text to answer questions. Point out that thinking about what they are reading as they read will make answering questions at the end of the story easier. Have students begin reading the selections on their own, answering the questions in the boxes and at the end of the selection.

Thinking Along on Tests

You have been thinking along as you read. Now practice thinking along to help you answer test questions.

Read and Think

- Read each selection.
- Stop at each box and answer the question.
- Answer the questions at the end of each selection.

Who is Shane?

Michael and Shane were never apart. Everywhere that Michael went, Shane was there, too.

Sometimes you would see Michael without Shane. Shane never came outside on rainy days. On partly cloudy days, he might come out. As soon as the sun disappeared, Shane was gone.

Michael liked Shane. He liked to play games, seeing how tall he could make Shane.

> **1** What are you thinking about now?

Possible Responses
Question 1

Sounds like they are good friends.

This response indicates that the student is drawing con-clusions from the text.

Why is Shane following him all around?

Encourage this student to try to make a statement about what he or she is thinking rather than asking a ques-tion.

I don't get it. It sounds like his shadow.

Although this student seems to be confused, he or she really has discovered the "twist" of the story. Reassure the student that as he or she continues to read, more information will make the story clearer.

Sometimes, though, Michael got tired of Shane. It was worse than having a little brother. Every time Michael took a step, Shane took a step. Michael sat down to rest, and Shane would sit, too. When Michael played ball, Shane always had to get into the game.

Michael tried to leave Shane behind one day. But he could not get away. Shane flattened himself against the buildings and sneaked along.

One day Michael was on his way to the park. Shane was tagging along. It seemed as if they were sewn together at the feet.

 2 What are you thinking about now?

Michael stopped to eat a frozen fruit bar. There was Shane eating one, too. Michael looked at his empty stick. It said, "You win a lucky wish!"

"Hooray!" Michael cried. "I wish that Shane would go home and stay!" He started off down the street. Soon he felt people looking at him. "Why are you staring?" Michael asked Ben and Ava.

63

The Selections and Questions

The three selections in this test section are of different types: one fictional story, one expository article, and one set of instructions. Each is followed by four multiple-choice questions and one short-answer question. The question format is typical of many standardized and criterion-referenced tests. The purpose-setting question format at the beginning of each selection is similar to that used on many nationally standardized tests. These questions help students to focus on a purpose for reading.

Possible Responses
Question 2

This is probably about somebody's shadow and there's going to be one missing when there's clouds.

This student has drawn conclusions based on the information in the story as well as prior knowledge.

This reminds me of my little brother.

This response is an example of a student using his or her personal experience to make connections while reading.

Michael won't be able to get rid of his shadow.

This student has made a prediction about what might happen next in the story.

"I'm not sure," Ben said, "but there's something strange about you today."

"Something's missing," Ava said, looking behind, beside, and in front of Michael. Ben and Ava left Michael to play alone.

Michael was lonely. He wished Shane were there to follow him when he danced down the sidewalk. He decided to go home and tell Shane he was sorry. Then he noticed a girl who looked very odd. She had two shadows, and one of them looked like a boy!

"Shane!" Michael cried. "Is that you?" It was, and Shane was happy that Michael had found him. The girl was very happy, too.

"That thing has been following us for an hour," she complained to her own shadow. It waved back at her. Michael took a huge step and a hop, checking to see that Shane was once again following along.

> **3** What are you thinking about now?

64

Possible Responses
Question 3

How could a shadow do that? This is a dumb story.

This is neat. I'd like to have two shadows.

I talk to my shadow sometimes. I think that's fun.

An unrealistic story like this one may provoke evaluative responses. As the students write, encourage them to just tell what they are thinking. Some reactions to the story may be negative, which does not make them any less valid than positive responses. Many kinds of responses demonstrate involvement with the text.

Darken the circle for the correct answer.

1. Michael can go outside without Shane on days when _____.
   - Ⓐ Shane is too tired to go
   - Ⓑ there is a ball game
   - Ⓒ Ben goes along
   - Ⓓ the sun is not shining

2. Michael got rid of Shane by _____.
   - Ⓐ sitting down to rest
   - Ⓑ making a lucky wish
   - Ⓒ sneaking away from him
   - Ⓓ talking to Ben and Ava

3. Where did Shane go when Michael sent him home?
   - Ⓐ to follow a little girl
   - Ⓑ to play ball with Ben
   - Ⓒ flat against the buildings
   - Ⓓ to look for rain

4. Shane is Michael's _____.
   - Ⓐ best friend
   - Ⓑ brother
   - Ⓒ shadow
   - Ⓓ toy

Write your answer on the lines below.

5. What happens in this story that could not really happen?

_____

_____

_____

_____

Answers and Analysis

1. D; inferential
2. B; literal
3. A; inferential
4. C; inferential
5. Evaluative/critical.

Correct responses include any of the following details from the story:

- You cannot make a wish that will cause your shadow to go away.
- The girl had two shadows.
- Shane could hear Michael talking.
- Shadows are not like real people.

Scoring Question 5:

2 = A response that describes something that could not have happened.

0 = A response showing that the student is unaware of the unreality of an event in the story.

Explanation of Comprehension Skills

Literal: The answer is specifically stated in the text.

Inferential: The answer can be inferred from the text, but it is not specifically stated.

Evaluative/Critical: The answer is based on an evaluation of the text.

Why are there falcons in our cities?

The peregrine is a kind of falcon. It had almost died off by the 1970s. There were only 39 pairs left. DDT was a poison that was used to kill insects. But the DDT stayed in the bodies of the small birds that ate the insects. When the peregrines ate the small birds, they also ate the poison. The poison made the shells of the eggs so thin that they broke. Also, horned owls were killing many peregrines. Scientists knew they needed to help the birds. They protected peregrine eggs until they could hatch. Laws were passed to stop the use of DDT.

 1 What are you thinking about now?

About the same time, some of these large, beautiful birds moved into big cities. They began living on tall buildings. There were no owls to attack them there. DDT was not used there. There were many pigeons for them to catch and eat.

Possible Responses
Question 1

DDT was very bad. Why did people use it at all?

This student has drawn a conclusion about a practice described in the text. In addition, the student asks a question rather than making a further comment. Encourage her or him to reread the first paragraph and then make a statement about why people once used DDT.

Why were the owls killing the birds?

This student demonstrates close reading and raises a good question that is left unaddressed by the text.

Why did they want to help those birds? There are so many birds in our field and we don't need more.

This student is demonstrating the strategy of using personal experience. He or she has also questioned the text. Ask, "Why do you think the scientists might have wanted to help the falcons?"

Scientists set special boxes on top of the buildings and put young peregrines in them. The scientists fed the birds, but the birds learned to catch food, too. A few landed in the streets, and people took them back up to their boxes.

The peregrines liked the city. They stayed there. Today they are flying around downtown Denver, New York, Baltimore, and other cities all over America. It is wonderful to look up at them soaring above the busy streets! The scientists did save the peregrines. Now there are 1,600 pairs!

> **2** What are you thinking about now?

67

Possible Responses
Question 2

I love birds. They can do all kinds of things I can't. We should save all the birds.

I wonder if we have those kinds of birds in our city.

It was nice that the people helped the birds.

These responses have shifted from asking questions to making opinionated conclusions. Note the progress of students' thinking as they proceed through a text.

Darken the circle for the correct answer.

6. A peregrine is a kind of _____.
   Ⓐ poison
   Ⓑ falcon
   Ⓒ owl
   Ⓓ scientist

7. One of the problems for the peregrine was _____.
   Ⓐ the poison DDT
   Ⓑ tall buildings
   Ⓒ pigeons
   Ⓓ boxes

8. Scientists might have to climb out on tall city buildings in order to _____.
   Ⓐ shoo the peregrines away
   Ⓑ save the pigeons
   Ⓒ help the peregrines
   Ⓓ clean the ledges

9. To the peregrine, the horned owl is _____.
   Ⓐ a friend
   Ⓑ a helper
   Ⓒ a good meal
   Ⓓ an enemy

Write your answer on the lines below.

10. How have scientists helped save the peregrines?

_____

_____

_____

_____

Answers and Analysis

6. B; literal
7. A; literal
8. C; inferential
9. D; evaluative/critical
10. Evaluative/critical.

Correct responses should list any of the following details from the story:
- Scientists protected the peregrine eggs.
- They helped the birds live in cities by placing special boxes on top of buildings and by putting young peregrines into them. When birds fell out, people returned them to their boxes.
- Scientists fed the birds.

Scoring Question 10:

2 = A good answer with discussion of how scientists helped the birds.

0 = A weak answer that does not provide an accurate example of how scientists helped the birds survive.

Explanation of Comprehension Skills

Literal: The answer is specifically stated in the text.
Inferential: The answer can be inferred from the text, but it is not specifically stated.
Evaluative/Critical: The answer is based on an evaluation of the text.

Help Name the Person of the Year!

It is time to name Person of the Year! Will it be someone from your class? You can suggest, or nominate, anyone. Think of a student who has done many things for our school this year.

Rosalie Hernandez was Person of the Year last year. She got Trevson Tree Company to plant trees in front of the school. Rosalie also won the city spelling bee.

 1 What are you thinking about now?

69

Possible Responses
Question 1

I wonder if a kid could be person of the year.

This response makes a prediction: that children as well as adults can become Person of the Year.

I think it should be called the student of the year.

This student has drawn a conclusion based on a close reading of details in the text.

I would like to win but I would not get picked.

This response shows a personal reaction to the information in the selection.

The same person cannot win two years in a row. So think of someone else to suggest this year. Here's what you need to do:

1. Get a nomination form from Mrs. Williams.
2. Name your choice for Person of the Year.
3. In 100 words or less, tell why that person should be Person of the Year.
4. Sign your name.
5. Turn in the form to Mrs. Williams by March 30.

You could become Person of the Year yourself, if someone else suggests you. Rosalie, Mrs. Williams, and Mr. Cookston will pick three persons from those you suggest. On April 14, all the students in the school will vote to decide who will be the Person of the Year.

 2 What are you thinking about now?

70

Possible Responses
Question 2

I think they will vote for the person who is the teacher's pet.

    This response indicates a personal connection to the selection and makes a prediction.

I thought the teachers would pick the winner.

    This student is interacting with the text by revising a prior prediction.

Will they give the winner any prizes?

    This student is making a prediction as well as questioning an issue left unaddressed by the text.

Darken the circle for the correct answer.

11. One thing Rosalie did was to

_____.

- Ⓐ get some trees planted
- Ⓑ help Mrs. Williams
- Ⓒ nominate a good friend
- Ⓓ win the math contest

12. What should you do if you want a friend to be Person of the Year?

- Ⓐ enter the spelling bee
- Ⓑ talk to Rosalie
- Ⓒ fill out a form
- Ⓓ pick three persons

13. Who makes the final decision about who will be Person of the Year?

- Ⓐ the whole school
- Ⓑ the fifth graders
- Ⓒ the students who were nominated
- Ⓓ Rosalie, Mrs. Williams, and Mr. Cookston

14. If you want to become Person of the Year, you need to _____.

- Ⓐ get a friend to turn in your name
- Ⓑ plant trees
- Ⓒ nominate yourself
- Ⓓ talk to Mr. Cookston and Rosalie

Write your answer on the lines below.

15. Why do you think the school has the rule that the same student cannot be Person of the Year twice?

_____

_____

_____

_____

71

Answers and Analysis

11. A; literal
12. C; literal
13. A; literal
14. A; inferential
15. Evaluative/critical.

Answers will vary, but might say that giving other students the chance to win is more fair than rewarding the same student twice.

Scoring Question 15:

2 = A good answer with a thoughtful/reasonable explanation of why the school has the rule.
0 = A weak answer that does not provide a reasonable explanation for the school policy.

Explanation of Comprehension Skills

Literal: The answer is specifically stated in the text.
Inferential: The answer can be inferred from the text, but it is not specifically stated.
Evaluative/Critical: The answer is based on an evaluation of the text.

Making Connections

Discussion

After the students have completed the questions for all three selections, discuss with them what they wrote in the boxes. Ask students to tell what they wrote in a box and to explain why they wrote what they did. Then, have students discuss how writing in the boxes helped them to remember what the selection was about so they could better answer the questions at the end of the selection.

For your own curricular planning, you might also want to review what students have written in the boxes. Reading what students have written will give you an idea of how well they are comprehending what they read and whether they need additional review of the process of thinking along as they read.

Scoring

Refer to the discussion of test taking on page T11 of the teacher's edition for information on scoring and interpreting student scores.

What Might Happen Next

Thinking About

What Might Happen Next

Read the story below. As you read, think about what might happen next.

The night was stormy and cold. Amy's whole family was in the kitchen. The windows rattled every time the wind blew. Then there was a loud BOOM. The lights went out. Amy's mother lit a candle. Her father gave them flashlights. Then there was a knock at the door. A man told them, "There is a chance of flooding here. Please go to the school. Hurry!"

Amy's family quickly packed some things. They stayed at the school until it was safe to go home. Was their house flooded? They were glad to see that it was safe.

72

Making and Revising Predictions

Readers constantly predict what is going to happen next when they read. A story develops in a reader's mind even before it is read on the page. Readers predict what characters will do, what they will say, and how a story might end. As they continue to read, readers review their predictions as they gather new information. The activities in this unit will help students to apply the strategy of making and revising predictions. This will help them to construct meaning as they read.

Introducing the Strategy

Have students create a group story. Begin with the phrase, "I was looking out my window one bright Saturday morning when I saw . . .," and have a student complete the sentence. Continue to have students build the story, as each student adds another sentence for the next student to complete. At the end, review the way the story evolved and discuss how and why it turned out the way it did. As they participate in this activity, students will realize that they have been making and revising predictions.

Applying the Strategy

Ask students to follow along as you read the story in the pupil book, or have a volunteer read it. Tell them to think about what is going to happen next as they read the story.

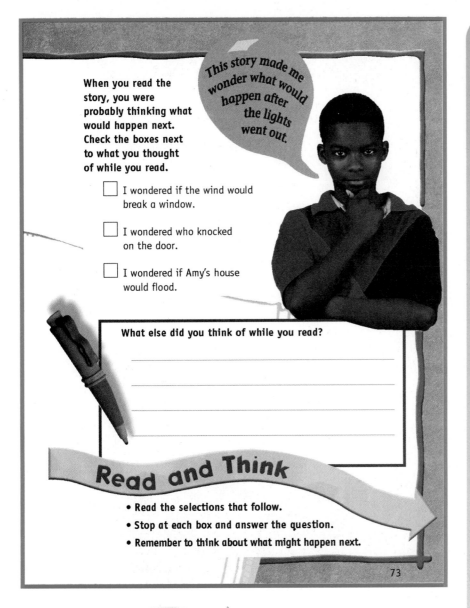

When you read the story, you were probably thinking what would happen next. Check the boxes next to what you thought of while you read.

This story made me wonder what would happen after the lights went out.

☐ I wondered if the wind would break a window.

☐ I wondered who knocked on the door.

☐ I wondered if Amy's house would flood.

What else did you think of while you read?

_____

_____

_____

Read and Think

• Read the selections that follow.

• Stop at each box and answer the question.

• Remember to think about what might happen next.

73

Read and Think

• Remind students that answering the questions in the boxes will help them think about the selections.

• Tell students that they may be using other strategies as they read, such as thinking about what they already know and how things are alike and different.

• Encourage students to think about what will happen next as they read the selections.

Discussing the Strategy

Have students complete the questions independently or as a group. Ask students what they were thinking about while the story was read. Ask questions such as the following:

• *What did you think made the loud boom?*

• *Why did the lights go out?*

Have students share their responses so that they can see the wide variety of predictions readers make as they read.

Explain to students that they will use this strategy as they read the selections in this unit.

Floss

Floss

By Kim Lewis

This selection is about a young sheepdog named Floss. Read the selection to find out the trouble Floss gets into and what she does next.

Floss was a young Border collie who belonged to an old man in a town. She walked with the old man in the streets and loved playing ball with children in the park.

"My son is a farmer," the old man told Floss. "He has a sheepdog who is too old to work. He needs a young dog to herd sheep on his farm. He could train a Border collie like you."

1   What do you think is going to happen?

74

Strategy Focus

Making and revising predictions to think about what happens next in a story.

Story at a Glance

This is a story about a sheep-dog named Floss who learns she can play after she has done her work.

Vocabulary

You may want to introduce the following words to your students:

heather   *shed*
drifting   *straying*

Getting Students Started

• Introducing the Selection

Ask students if they have ever had a pet that learned tricks or had special talents. Ask them if they are familiar with any dogs that are trained to work as Seeing Eye dogs or guard dogs. Ask if they have seen sheepdogs herding sheep. Then ask, "What might happen if a Seeing Eye dog or a guard dog went off to play instead of doing its job?" Tell them to think about what happens to Floss in this story and what they think is going to happen next.

• Purpose for Reading

Students read to find out what happens to Floss.

Possible Responses

Question 1

Floss is going to go to the farm and take care of sheep.

This response makes a valid prediction that reflects an accurate reading of the story. Encourage such responses.

She wouldn't like to take care of sheep.

Like the previous response, this response makes a prediction. However, this student is anticipating how Floss will react to working with the sheep. The student is empathizing with Floss based on what he or she has already read.

I never heard of a sheepdog.

In this response, the student is questioning the content of the story. Take this opportunity to discuss sheepdogs: what they are, what they do, and why they are a special type of dog. Encourage this student to predict what might happen next in the story by asking, "What do you think the old man might have Floss do?"

So Floss and the old man traveled, away from the town with its streets and houses and children playing ball in the park.

They came to the heather-covered hills of a valley, where nothing much grew except sheep.

 2 How do you think Floss will feel about working with the sheep?

Somewhere in her memory, Floss knew about sheep. Old Nell soon showed her how to round them up. The farmer trained her to run wide and lie down, to walk on behind, to shed, and to pen. She worked very hard to become a good sheepdog.

 75

Strategy Tip

Emphasize to students that they should try to make predictions—telling what they think is going to happen next in the story—as they answer the questions in the boxes.

Possible Responses
Question 2

She'll try to play with them.
This is a good response that makes a prediction based on events earlier in the story.

She won't like the sheep.
This response is another example of a student anticipating how the dog will feel. Students often put themselves in the place of the story characters, even if the characters are not human. This strategy helps students empathize with the characters and better understand the story.

I think she's gonna miss the kids.
In this response, the student refers back to an earlier part of the story in anticipating future events.

Use this activity to reinforce using background knowledge. Organize students into pairs. Ask each pair to discuss the pets they have, or the pets or working animals owned by a friend or acquaintance. Have students make a chart or a Venn diagram that illustrates what one of the animals discussed does for work and for play.

But sometimes Floss woke up at night, while Nell lay sound asleep. She remembered playing with children and rounding up balls in the park.

The farmer took Floss up to the hill one day to see if she could gather the sheep on her own. She was rounding them up when she heard a sound. At the edge of the field, the farmer's children were playing with a brand-new black-and-white ball.

 3 Now how do you think Floss will feel about working with the sheep?

76

Possible Responses
Question 3

She isn't going to want to work.
This is a good response that gives a direct answer to the question. Ask this student to follow up his or her response by telling what he or she thinks is going to happen next.

She wants to play with the kids back in the town.
This response refers to an earlier part of the text. Recalling and restating text are both important reading strategies. To clarify the difference between what Floss wants to do and how she feels, ask, "How do you think Floss feels when she sees the children playing?"

I don't know what the sheep will do.
Sometimes a response appears to miss the point of the question. This student may be anticipating how the sheep will react to Floss. You can stress the subject of the question, Floss, by asking, "What do you think Floss is thinking about when she is working with the sheep? How do you think she feels?"

Floss remembered all about children. She ran to play with their ball. She showed off her best nose kicks, her best passes. She did her best springs in the air.

"Hey, Dad, look at this!" yelled the children. "Look at Floss!"

The sheep started drifting away. The sheep escaped through the gate and into the yard. There were sheep in the garden and sheep on the road.

"FLOSS! LIE DOWN!" The farmer's voice was like thunder. "You are supposed to work on this farm, not play!"

He took Floss back to the doghouse.

> **4** What do you think is going to happen to Floss?

77

Possible Responses
Question 4

Floss is going to be very unhappy.

Students often respond with statements about attitudes, beliefs, or feelings. In this case, the prediction refers to how a character will feel rather than what the character will do or what events will happen. This is a good prediction, but ask, "What do you think the farmer will do now?"

I would not want to be Floss.

This student is empathizing with Floss. Ask, "Why would you not want to be Floss? What do you think might happen to her?"

I think the farmer will make Floss do more work.

In this response, the student anticipates how a different character in the story will react. This kind of prediction indicates attention to all characters, not just the main character, and it reflects a good understanding of the story.

Floss lay and worried about balls and sheep. She dreamed about the streets of a town, the hills of a valley, children and farmers, all mixed together, while Nell had to round up the straying sheep.

But Nell was too old to work every day, and Floss had to learn to take her place. She worked so hard to gather sheep well that she was too tired to dream any more. The farmer was pleased and ran Floss in the dog trials.

 5   What do you think is going to happen to Nell?

Possible Responses
Question 5

....

Maybe Old Nell will help Floss.

In this response, the student may be recalling that initially Floss helped Nell. You can follow up on the student's response by asking, "What might Nell do to help?"

Old Nell will not be able to work.

This is a good response that builds on information provided in the text. The student is thinking that because Nell is too old to work every day, she will soon be unable to work at all.

Nell might learn to play ball with the children.

In this response, the student is synthesizing information from the story (Nell does not know about children and play) with a creative prediction.

"She's a good worker now," the old man said.
The children still wanted to play with their ball.
"Hey, Dad," they asked, "can Old Nell play now?"
But Nell didn't know about children and play.
"No one can play ball like Floss," they said.
So the farmer gave it some thought.

> 6   Now what do you think is going to happen to Floss?

79

Have students draw and label pictures of themselves at work and at play. Discuss with students how their experiences at work and at play are similar to or different from the experiences of working animals such as Floss.

Possible Responses
Question 6

Do you think he is going to get another working dog?
When a student writes a question, it indicates that he or she may be confused or may be thinking at a higher level about the story. Ask, "What do you think will happen to Floss next?" and also have the student answer his or her own question.

She's gonna play and work.
This is a logical prediction in which the student asserts that both work and play are important to Floss.

Maybe he will let Floss play one more time.
In this prediction, the student is showing comprehension of what is important to Floss and is hoping that the farmer is good-natured.

It is very important to have students discuss what they have written in the boxes to help them use the strategy of making predictions.

Discussing the Think-Alongs

- Give as many students as possible a chance to tell what they have written in one of the boxes.
- When students explain their responses, be sure to point out when they were making predictions and revising earlier predictions.
- Ask students how making predictions helped them understand the story better.

Reteaching

For those students who have not written or are having difficulty with the activity:

- Ask students to summarize what happened and tell what they were thinking about as they read.
- Model your use of prediction by telling what you thought might happen to Floss at different points in the story.
- Ask questions that motivate students to think about predictions, such as the following:
  - *What did you think Floss was going to do when she first got to the farm?*
  - *What did you think Nell was going to do after Floss arrived?*
  - *After Floss let the sheep get away, what did you think the farmer would do?*

"Go on, then," he whispered to Floss.

The children kicked the ball high into the air.

Floss remembered all about children. She ran to play with their ball. She showed off her best nose kicks, her best passes. She did her best springs in the air. And they all played ball together.

 7 What do you think Floss will do from now on?

80

Possible Responses
Question 7

She'll keep playing ball with the kids.

This student uses information from the selection to predict what Floss will do. Ask, "Do you think she will keep working, too?"

Floss will take good care of the sheep and play with Nell and play with the kids too.

In this response, the student makes a prediction and states an opinion that Floss is a good caretaker of sheep.

Maybe Floss will go to school with the kids and learn new tricks. Maybe she'll bring the sheep to school.

This student has made an imaginative prediction about what might happen next to Floss. Encourage the student to think about what he or she has already read to make a more plausible prediction. Ask, "Do you think the farmer will let Floss go to school? Do you think the teachers will allow Floss and the sheep to go to school?"

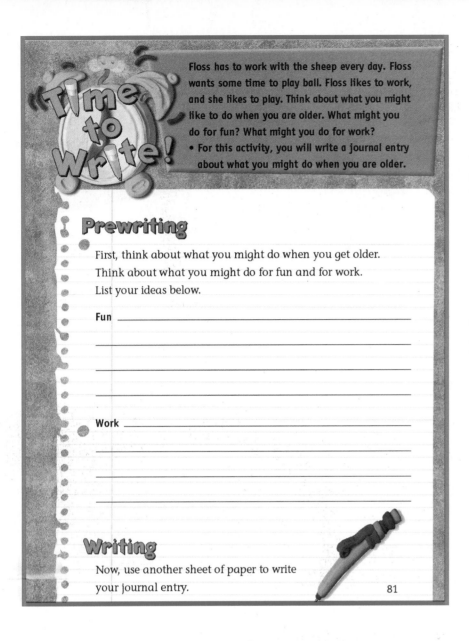

"Time to Write!"

Floss has to work with the sheep every day. Floss wants some time to play ball. Floss likes to work, and she likes to play. Think about what you might like to do when you are older. What might you do for fun? What might you do for work?

• For this activity, you will write a journal entry about what you might do when you are older.

Prewriting

First, think about what you might do when you get older. Think about what you might do for fun and for work. List your ideas below.

Fun _____

_____

_____

_____

Work _____

_____

_____

_____

_____

Writing

Now, use another sheet of paper to write your journal entry.

81

Prewriting

Explain that the prewriting activity will help students organize their thoughts so they can write a journal entry to themselves. They will list things they plan to do for fun and for work when they are older.

Writing

Remind students that their journal entries should be written clearly so that when they read them years from now they will understand the ideas that they had as youths.

Sharing

When students have finished the writing activity, organize them into groups of two or three. Have them read their journal entries to each other and discuss what they would like to do for work and play when they are older.

Making Connections

Activity Links

- Have students collect pictures, stories, and books about animals at work and at play. Set up a display, such as a collage or a bulletin board, with the title, "Animals at Work and Animals at Play."
- Organize students into groups and ask them to talk about animals they own or are familiar with: household pets, zoo animals, or farm animals. Have the students draw the animals at work or at play.
- Have a discussion about animals trained to help people. If possible, arrange a classroom visit by someone with a guide dog or a service animal.

Reading Links

You might want to include these books in a discussion about animals that help people:

- **Hugger to the Rescue** by Dorothy Hinshaw Patent (Dutton, 1994).
- **Ice Horse** by Candace Christiansen (Dial, 1993).
- **Animals Who Have Won Our Hearts** by Jean Craighead George (HarperCollins, 1994).
- **In the Village of the Elephants** by Jeremy Schmidt (Walker, 1994).

Gail Devers: A Runner's Dream

Strategy Focus

Making and revising predictions to think about what happens next in a story.

Story at a Glance

After training for years, a female runner overcomes a debilitating disease to win two gold medals in the Olympics.

Vocabulary

You may want to introduce the following words to your students:

sprinter   hurdles
jogged   stadium

Getting Students Started

• Introducing the Selection

Ask students to think about something they would like to achieve very much. Ask "What might you do to achieve your goal?" Tell students that the hero of this story is Gail Devers, a young woman who had high goals. Ask students to suggest qualities that might help someone like Gail achieve a goal.

• Purpose for Reading

Students read to find out how Gail Devers became a winner.

Gail Devers: A Runner's Dream

By Katherine Mead

You are about to read a true story. It is about a woman who always wanted to be the best at what she did. She had to get through some hard times first. Read the selection to find out how Gail Devers became a champion.

Becoming a Winner

Do you ever dream of being the best in the world at something? You might be the best singer, basketball player, or tennis player. What would you like to be?

This is the story of a woman who has always wanted to be the best. Gail Devers is a famous runner who trained many years to become a winner. She has won two gold medals in the Olympics. It was not easy for her to do this, but she kept trying until she did.

 1   How do you think Gail Devers became a winner?

82

Possible Responses
Question 1

She tried real hard.
  This is a short answer, but it reflects a close reading of the story. The text clearly states that Gail kept trying until she succeeded.

I don't know but I'm going to find out.
  This response shows an understanding that the text will provide an answer to the question. To encourage this student to make a prediction, ask, "What do you think Gail will do to become a winner?" Emphasize to the student that the question may have several correct answers and that he or she can make a guess.

She must have practiced a lot of running.
  This response shows the use of background knowledge. The student knows that someone can improve a skill by practicing.

Gail Devers grew up in California. Her father was a minister, and her mother was a teacher's aide. Gail and her big brother liked to swim and ride bikes together. Gail loved to be active.

Gail was a good student. When she was in high school, Gail found something she was really good at doing. She could run really fast.

Gail's high school didn't have a track team. There was no one to teach her about running and winning races. She had to learn on her own.

Strategy Tip

Tell students to focus on predictions—using what has already taken place in the story to tell what will happen next—in responding to the questions.

83

Gail became a very good sprinter. A sprint is a short, very fast race. Gail's best sprint was the 100-meter dash. This is a little longer than a football field.

Gail also learned to run in races that have hurdles to jump over. Hurdles are gates about as high as a kitchen counter. A runner jumps over ten hurdles while sprinting as fast as she can.

Before long, Gail was racing against the best high school girls in the country. She was still training on her own, without a coach.

 2 What are you thinking about now?

84

Possible Responses
Question 2

I'd be scared I'd trip over it.
This response shows that the student is both drawing from personal experience and visualizing events in the story.

Maybe she doesn't need a coach. She's doing it by herself.
This response demonstrates an understanding of the story. To encourage a more thoughtful response, ask, "How might having a coach help Gail become an even better runner?"

If she gets a coach I bet she will do even better.
This response shows that the student is both making a prediction and using background knowledge about the role that a coach plays in an athlete's success.

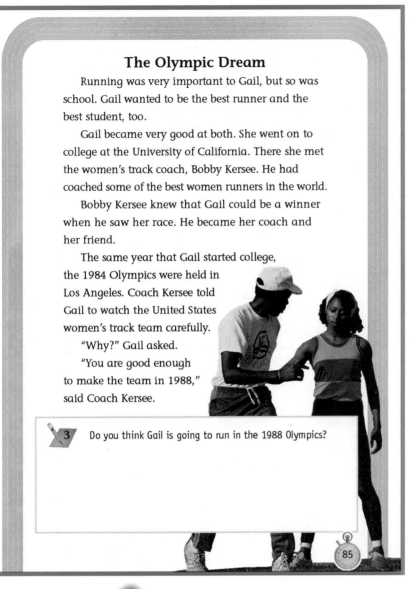

The Olympic Dream

Running was very important to Gail, but so was school. Gail wanted to be the best runner and the best student, too.

Gail became very good at both. She went on to college at the University of California. There she met the women's track coach, Bobby Kersee. He had coached some of the best women runners in the world.

Bobby Kersee knew that Gail could be a winner when he saw her race. He became her coach and her friend.

The same year that Gail started college, the 1984 Olympics were held in Los Angeles. Coach Kersee told Gail to watch the United States women's track team carefully.

"Why?" Gail asked.

"You are good enough to make the team in 1988," said Coach Kersee.

3 Do you think Gail is going to run in the 1988 Olympics?

85

Possible Responses
Question 3

....

She always wants to be the best so I guess she'll do it.

This response not only shows an understanding of the details of the story, but also uses that information to support a conclusion.

The coach thinks she can do it.

This response provides important information but does not directly answer the question. Ask, "Do you agree with the coach's prediction? Why or why not?"

The story said she wins some medals.

This response reflects a close reading of the story. You might attempt to elicit a response about the narrative rather than just the introduction. For example, ask, "How do you think Gail was able to win two medals?"

Gail saw the great runners and wanted to be a part of the Olympics. She worked hard and won many races. In 1987, she ran the 100-meter dash in just under 11 seconds. That was close to a world record!

 4 What are you thinking about now?

Possible Responses
Question 4
....

I'm pretty fast too.
This response is a brief but strong statement showing a personal reaction to the text. The student has formed a personal attachment to Gail Devers.

11 seconds seems like a good time.
This response shows an understanding of the mood and details of the story.

That's like that other guy.
This response is unclear. To get the student to clarify, ask, "Are you thinking of another fast runner?"

Coach Kersee was excited. "Once Gail sees what she can do, no one can stop her!" he said.

In 1988, Gail Devers was chosen for the U.S. Olympic team. She was making her dream come true. Gail wanted to show she was the best sprinter and best hurdler. But something was wrong.

Gail didn't know why, but she wasn't feeling her best. She was having a hard time running races. She was running slower than she had in high school. No one was sure what was wrong, but Gail didn't get any better. Gail found it was harder and harder to race.

 5 Now tell whether you think Gail will run in the 1988 Olympics.

87

Possible Responses
Question 5

It said she wins in the Olympics.

This response shows that the student recalled what was stated in the beginning of the story. Recalling and restating text are important reading strategies.

I don't think she's going to run anymore.

This response reflects a good understanding of the story and may be an example of revising a prediction based on new information.

What is wrong with her?

This response shows an understanding that something must be affecting Gail's performance. To help the student answer the question, ask, "What could be wrong with her? Do you think that might keep her from running in the 1988 Olympics?"

Gail Gets Sick

Gail got worse instead of better. Every race was harder than the one before. Soon she couldn't see with her left eye. She had headaches, she lost weight, and her body shook. Her doctors couldn't find out what was wrong.

Gail had to stop running. Her feet hurt her so badly that her family had to carry her around. But Gail never gave up hope. She studied hard and finished college at the University of California.

At last in 1990, doctors found that Gail had a serious illness called Grave's disease. Her doctors weren't even sure that she would live.

Gail's doctors found a medicine that helped her. By the spring of 1991, Gail began to feel better. She started to walk again. No one thought she'd be able to run. But Gail and Coach Kersee knew she would run again.

 6 What do you think will happen?

Possible Responses
Question 6

How is she going to be able to do that?

This response shows an understanding of the difficulty of recovering from a serious illness. To encourage a more direct response to the question, ask, "Do you think Gail will be able to run again?"

I bet they are going to be right about that.

This response shows that the student is making a prediction. To elicit a more detailed response, ask, "Why do you think Gail and Coach Kersee are right about Gail running again?"

My brother got sick too but he took medicine that made him better just like this lady.

This response shows that the student is using background knowledge and is relating the story to personal experience.

Gail came back one step at a time. First she walked, then she jogged in socks, and finally she ran. Under Coach Kersee's careful eye, Gail Devers began sprinting again. Some said it was a miracle. Gail said it was because she believed in herself. Coach Kersee believed in her, too.

The 1992 Olympic Games were one year away. It was a short time for Gail to get ready. She had to work very hard.

Ask students to talk about something they are good at. Have students write about themselves and what they are good at, or have them draw pictures with labels and captions. Make a board display for the classroom or hallway with the pictures drawn by the students.

Gail knew she could make it. She took her medicine, rested, and ate well. Then she began to run in races again. Soon Gail won some big races. At the Olympic trials, Gail was great in the 100-meter dash and 100-meter hurdles.

 7 What are you thinking about now?

Coach Kersee had said that when Gail made up her mind to do something, she did it. Gail made the 1992 Olympic team. She would go to Barcelona, Spain. She had reached another goal.

90

Possible Responses
Question 7

She really got better.
This response suggests that the student was surprised by Gail's recovery. You might ask how well the student thinks Gail will do in the Olympics now that she has recovered from her illness.

I'd like to be famous like Gail Devers.
This student is responding personally to the story and is identifying with Gail Devers' success.

I don't think I could do that.
This student is relating personal experience to the story, and is also stating an opinion about his or her own abilities compared with those of Gail Devers.

Going for the Gold

At the Olympics, Gail was set to run the 100-meter dash and the 100-meter hurdles. Everyone thought she'd win the hurdles.

People did not think she could win the 100-meter dash because she had been so sick. She surprised everyone. Gail ran her fastest race ever, with a time of 10.82 seconds. That's about how long it takes to start a car!

8 What do you think Gail will do in her next race?

She won a gold medal. When she got her medal, everyone in the stadium stood up and cheered for her. Coach Kersee and Gail's family cheered the loudest. They knew she was a great hero.

Gail was hoping to win a second gold medal for the 100-meter hurdles. She thought this was her best race.

91

Possible Responses
Question 8

Everybody said she's the best at the other race so she's supposed to win.

This response is a thoughtful prediction that links two earlier parts of the story.

The story said she wins two medals.

This response shows good recall of information presented at the beginning of the story.

Maybe she'll get sick again or something.

This is a logical prediction, even though the story is optimistic about Gail's recovery.

It is very important to have students discuss what they have written in the boxes to help them focus on what they think might happen next.

Discussing the Think-Alongs

- Ask students to tell what they were thinking when they wrote in the boxes.
- Ask students how predicting what might happen helped them think about the story.
- Have students tell whether they revised any of their predictions as they read further in the story.

Reteaching

For those students who have not written or are having difficulty with the activity:

- Ask them to tell what they were thinking about as they read.
- Model your own strategy for making predictions as you read the story. Emphasize that your predictions might change as you read the story.
- Ask questions about what could happen next in the story and how predictions can help students better understand what they are reading, such as the following:
  - *How do you think that Gail's illness affected her running?*
  - *What happened after Gail got better?*
  - *What happened after Gail ran and won at the Olympics?*

During the race, things didn't go the way she'd hoped. Gail started with a big lead. As she was about to cross the finish line, she tripped on the last hurdle. Four other runners came in before her. She didn't win, but she did finish the race. Gail said, "I'll be back next time. The word *quit* is not in my vocabulary."

 9 What do you think Gail will do next?

In 1996, Gail Devers won another gold medal at the Olympics in Atlanta, Georgia. She had done it. She had become the best. Sometimes dreams take a little time to come true.

Possible Responses
Question 9

She's going to keep running.
This is a logical prediction based on the previous events in the story.

Maybe she's going to do something else.
This response also predicts what Gail will do. It doesn't matter if the prediction is correct. The goal of the strategy is to make predictions.

What's she doing now?
This response shows that the student is attempting to visualize Gail's life after the Olympics. To elicit a more elaborate response, ask, "What do you think Gail might be doing now, as a former champion?"

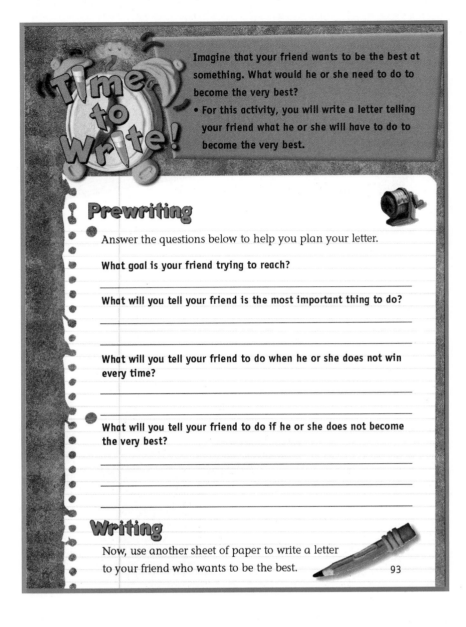

"Time to Write!"

Imagine that your friend wants to be the best at something. What would he or she need to do to become the very best?

- For this activity, you will write a letter telling your friend what he or she will have to do to become the very best.

Prewriting

Answer the questions below to help you plan your letter.

What goal is your friend trying to reach?

_____

What will you tell your friend is the most important thing to do?

_____

_____

What will you tell your friend to do when he or she does not win every time?

_____

_____

What will you tell your friend to do if he or she does not become the very best?

_____

_____

_____

Writing

Now, use another sheet of paper to write a letter to your friend who wants to be the best.

93

Prewriting

Explain that the prewriting activity will help students organize their thoughts about how they can be a good coach and help someone be the best he or she can be. This will help the students when they write letters advising the person they are coaching.

Writing

Remind students that their letter should help the person strive to do his or her best, whether he or she is an artist, musician, speaker, or athlete.

Sharing

When students have finished writing their letters, have students gather in pairs and take turns reading their letters to each other. Partners can provide feedback about whether the coaching advice will help the person succeed.

Making Connections

Activity Links

- Have students design posters to help inspire other people to work as hard as Gail Devers did. Display students' work in the classroom or in a school hallway.
- Have students use the library to find out what inspired other famous people who achieved their goals.
- Have students explore other Olympic events and champions.

Reading Links

You might want to include the following readings in a discussion of inspirational people:

- **Susan Butcher, Sled Dog Racer** by Ginger Wadsworth (Lerner Publications, 1994).
- Issues of the magazine, "Sports Illustrated for Kids."
- **Hearts of Gold: A Celebration of Special Olympics and Its Heroes** by Sheila Dinn (Blackbirch, 1996).

Abe Lincoln's Hat

Strategy Focus

Making and revising predictions to think about what happens next in a story.

Story at a Glance

A lawyer who stores his important papers in his hat becomes a great president.

Vocabulary

You may want to introduce the following words to your students:

lawyer   argument
handkerchief   leather
courthouse

Getting Students Started

- **Introducing the Selection**

Ask students if they have heard of Abe Lincoln. Students may know that he was a president of the United States. Students may also know that his profile is on the penny and that his picture is on the five-dollar bill. You can also talk with students about Lincoln's childhood on the midwestern frontier.

- **Purpose for Reading**

Students read to learn about Abe Lincoln's life and the role his tall hat plays in this story.

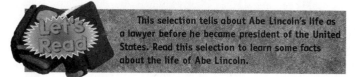

Abe Lincoln's Hat
By Martha Brenner

This selection tells about Abe Lincoln's life as a lawyer before he became president of the United States. Read this selection to learn some facts about the life of Abe Lincoln.

Abe Lincoln didn't have much money. But when he became a lawyer, he wanted to look his best. He bought a long black coat and a tall black hat. Every day Abe wore his hat to his new job. People noticed the tall man in the tall hat. He was friendly to everyone. When they needed a lawyer, they remembered him.

94

Possible Responses
Question 1

Abe Lincoln's new job.
   This response is brief, but it reflects the student's understanding of the text and makes a prediction.

It's going to be about how Lincoln freed the slaves.
   This is a high-level response that makes a prediction and applies background knowledge about Abraham Lincoln.

Abe Lincoln's Hat is a silly title.
   This response is not a prediction but a commentary on the text. Responses like this show that the student is thinking about the text. To encourage the student to make a prediction, ask "Do you think the hat will be important in the story?"

Abe lived in Illinois. His state was mostly wilderness. Then more and more settlers came. They built houses and farms and new towns.

Sometimes they didn't get along. They argued over land and animals and money. Lawyers like Abe could help people settle their arguments. They could help people get a fair trial in court.

 1 What do you think this story will be about?

Abe Lincoln was a smart lawyer. People came to him with all kinds of problems. He helped them all. But he had one problem himself. He forgot to answer letters. He forgot where he put important papers. A good lawyer cannot forget. Abe wanted to be a good lawyer, but he was not a good paper-keeper. What could he do?

 2 What do you think Abe could do?

Strategy Tip

Emphasize the importance of making predictions—using what has already taken place in the story to tell what will happen next—in responding to the questions.

Possible Responses
Question 2

take better care of his papers
This is a good response that directly addresses the question, even though it is not a complete sentence.

I forgot to put my socks on once.
While this response does not respond to the question, it does relate personal experiences to the text. Ask, "What do you think Abe could do about his forgetfulness?"

I write things down to remember them. If he wrote things down he'd remember them.
This response shows a student's personal connection to the text and demonstrates critical thinking.

Abe had an idea. His tall hat! He could push letters deep inside it. He could stuff notes into the leather band. When he took off his hat, the papers would remind him what he had to do. The idea worked, most of the time.

One day some boys played a trick on Abe. They tied a string across the street. They strung it way up high. Everyone in town could walk under it. Everyone except Abe.

When Abe walked down the street, the string knocked off his hat. Papers flew everywhere! He bent over to pick them up. The boys ran out of hiding. They jumped all over him. Abe laughed. He was not mad at the boys. He liked a good joke. But the trick did not stop him from carrying papers in his hat!

3 What are you thinking about now?

96

Possible Responses
Question 3

Abe was taller than everyone in town.

This student is making an inference—stating something that was not directly stated in the text. This is an extremely important reading strategy.

Good trick!

This brief response is a genuine reaction to the trick played on Abe. Encourage the student to elaborate.

I never heard of keeping papers in a hat.

This response shows a personal reaction to a unique aspect of the text—keeping valuable papers in one's hat for safekeeping.

Once a lawyer sent Abe a letter. Abe stuck it in his hat. The next day, Abe bought a new hat. He put away his old one. Weeks later the lawyer wrote again: "Why didn't you answer my letter?" Then Abe remembered. The letter was still in his old hat!

Many towns in Illinois had no lawyers and no judges. So every spring and fall, a judge and some lawyers traveled from town to town. Abe went too. He packed his hat with papers, his checkbook, and a handkerchief.

At the head of the parade of lawyers rode the judge. No one could miss him. He weighed over 300 pounds. Two horses pulled his buggy.

Abe's horse was skinny and slow. His name was Old Buck. Abe and Old Buck traveled lonely country roads. In the snow. In the rain. In the mud.

4 What was Abe going to do when he traveled?

Possible Responses
Question 4

The hat didn't help him remember to do things.

This response shows that the student is thinking about the text. Tell the student, "That's a good point. Now, what was Abe going to do when he traveled?"

He was going to help the fat judge.

This response directly answers the question and shows that the student understands the story.

What's a buggy?

This response indicates confusion. Have the student look up buggy in a dictionary. Sometimes, however, students may query the meaning of a detail when they are confused about a difficult concept. You may want to review any ideas the student is having trouble with in the story.

Ask students
to compare and
contrast the lawyers and the
judge in this section. Have them
discuss the similarities and differences between the way the
lawyers had to travel and the way
the judge had to travel. Also have
them compare the roles that the
lawyers and the judge played in
courts in this section.

Traveling made Abe very tired. He dreamed of a soft bed and a good meal. But the lawyers had to stay at poor country inns. The food was bad. The rooms were cold. The beds were crawling with bugs. The lawyers had to share beds. Except the judge. He had his own bed.

5 What are you thinking about now?

Early in the morning the courthouse bell would ring. Abe hurried to court. Pigs lived under one courthouse. Abe had to talk loudly over the grunts and squeals.

People came from near and far to hear Abe. He made trials easy to understand. He told jokes and stories. People said he could make a cat laugh.

Once Abe whispered a joke to another lawyer. The lawyer laughed out loud. "Quiet!" the judge yelled. "You are fined five dollars." When the trial was over, the judge asked to hear the joke. He laughed as hard as the lawyer. "That was worth five dollars," he said. "Forget the fine."

98

Possible Responses
Question 5

My brothers have bunk beds.
This student is connecting to the story using personal experience. Encourage the student to expand on his or her response by asking, "How is your brothers' bedroom similar or different from the inns where Abe stayed?"

I wouldn't like to stay there.
This response shows personal involvement with the text. The student has expressed an opinion and responded as if he or she were part of the group traveling together in the text.

Those were hard times for Abe.
In this response, the student empathizes with Abe's discomfort at the inns where he stays.

At another trial two men argued over who owned a young horse. Each said he owned the mother of the colt. Abe led everyone outside. He put the two grown horses on one side of the lawn. He held the colt on the other side. Then he set the colt free. It headed straight to its real mother!

6 How did telling jokes and stories help Abe?

One day Abe got a letter. It was from Hannah Armstrong. Years before, Abe had lived with her family. Mrs. Armstrong cooked for Abe. She sewed up the holes in his pants.

99

Possible Responses
Question 6

He made trials easy to understand.

This student has directly quoted a line from the text. Although this is a valid response, it is not clear that the student understands the question or passage. Say, "Yes, that's a good point. How else do you think telling jokes helped Abe?"

Abe made people laugh, even the judge.

This student clearly indicates the cause-and-effect relationship between Abe's ability to tell jokes and make people laugh. Encourage this student to clarify this connection by asking, "How did making people laugh help Abe?"

Why was it funny that Abe helped the colt find its mother?

This student is focusing on only one paragraph to answer the question. Encourage the student to reread the entire passage, and ask, "How do you think that Abe's use of jokes helped him in the courtroom?"

Now she begged Abe for help. Her son Duff was in jail—for murder! Abe did not stick this letter in his hat. He wrote back right away: "Of course I'll help you."

Duff had been in a big fight. It was very dark. But a man said he saw Duff kill someone. Duff said he did not do it. Abe believed Duff. But how could he prove that the man was wrong—or lying?

 7 What will Abe do to help Duff?

"How could you see in the dark?" Abe asked the man.

"The moon was full," the man said. "It was bright as day."

"Are you sure the moon was full?" Abe asked again and again.

"Yes," the man repeated.

Then Abe held up a famous book of facts. It said there was NO moon in the sky at the time of the fight! Now no one believed the man anymore. The judge set Duff free!

100

Possible Responses
Question 7

Abe proves Duff didn't do it.
This response makes a logical prediction. Ask the student to predict how Abe will prove Duff didn't kill the other person.

What if Duff really did it?
This response reflects a close reading of the text and demonstrates strong critical thinking skills.

I think he'll make it turn out OK.
This response makes a prediction, although it is vague. Encourage this student to be more specific by asking, "How is Abe going to make it turn out OK? How will this help Duff?"

Abe believed slavery was wrong. His state had laws against it. But the laws were not clear. Many blacks were treated like slaves. Nance was one of them. She worked for a storekeeper who sold her to another man. This man treated Nance badly. So she would not work for him.

Abe argued for Nance in court. Illinois was a free state, he said. All its people are free, whatever their color. The judge decided Abe was right. From then on, no one could be bought or sold in Illinois.

ESOL

Organize students into pairs or groups whose members share a language other than English. Ask each pair or group to pick out some key words in the story (e.g., *lawyer, judge, buggy, horse, letter, joke*). Have students then write the same words in their own language. Sometimes the English and non-English words may be similar. Students may also see that some English words are borrowed from other languages. If there are several languages represented in your classroom, students may also see that some non-English languages are similar.

Abe had saved Nance. But half the states in America still had slaves. In a few years there would be new states out west. Abe did not want slavery to spread to these states.

Abe tried to get elected to the U.S. Senate. If he won, he could make laws to stop slavery. He ran against Stephen Douglas. Douglas argued that each state should decide for itself if it wanted slaves. They gave speeches all over Illinois. Thousands of people heard them. Abe lost the election but became famous.

> **8** What do you think Abe will do next?

Possible Responses
Question 8

He should run again.
This student's response shows use of background knowledge about voting and elections.

He will try to stop slavery.
This response is an opinion and indicates use of background knowledge as well as prediction.

I knew Duff didn't kill anyone.
This response confirms the student's belief about what he or she expected to happen earlier in the story. Verifying or revising predictions is an important reading strategy. Ask the student to make a prediction about what Abe might do after losing the election.

In 1860, Abe ran for president. Stephen Douglas ran too. This time Abe won.

Abe grew a beard for his new job. He took his family to Washington. At every train station, crowds cheered the new president.

Abe was ready to make his first speech as president. He carried a cane, a tall silk hat, and his speech. He looked for a place to put his hat.

Stephen Douglas stepped up. "If I can't be president," he said, "I can at least hold his hat."

It is very important to have the students read and discuss what they have written in the boxes about what they think might happen next.

Discussing the Think-Alongs

- Ask students to explain what they were thinking about when they wrote in the boxes.
- Ask students how predicting what they think will happen next can help them understand the story.
- Have students tell whether they revised any of their predictions as they read further in the story.

Reteaching

For those students who have not written or are having difficulty with the activity:

- Ask them to tell what they were thinking about as they read and how this changed as they continued reading.
- Model your own use of prediction by sharing what you think will happen next in the story.
- Ask questions to help the students predict what will happen next in the story, such as the following:
  - *How do you make guesses about what will happen next in a story?*
  - *How do questions in the text of a story help you think about what will happen next?*
  - *Do you change your predictions as you read?*

Abe Lincoln was a great president. He freed the slaves. He worked for fair laws. He helped unite the nation after a long war. But he never changed his ways. He always kept important papers in his tall hat!

9   What are you thinking about now?

104

Possible Responses
Question 9

Abe Lincoln was the president.
This response restates the text. Encourage the student to give additional details.

Was Stephen Douglas his friend now?
Posing questions is a typical response for some students. Asking them to answer their own questions encourages them to think more deeply about the text.

I was wondering if the hat was going to come back into the story.
This response is an excellent comment on the story and shows that the student may have been verifying a prediction about the role of the hat.

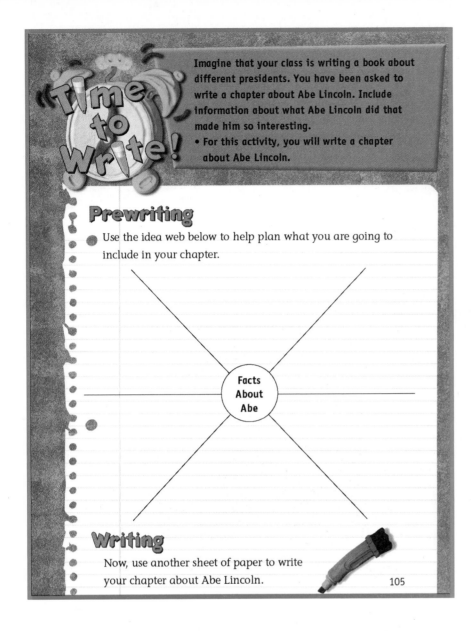

Making Connections

Activity Links

- Have students research another president of their choice and compare him to Abe Lincoln.
- Have students act out one episode from the book and present it at a school assembly or to another class.
- Ask students to imagine that their community has a serious problem. Then, have them write a letter to Abe Lincoln asking for his help or advice.

Reading Links

You might want to include these biographies in a discussion of Abe Lincoln and other famous people in American history:

- **And Then What Happened, Paul Revere?** by Jean Fritz (Coward McCann, 1998).
- **Where Do You Think You're Going, Christopher Columbus?** by Jean Fritz (Putnam, 1980).
- **Lincoln: A Photobiography** by Russell Freedman (Clarion, 1989).
- **Abe Lincoln: Log Cabin to White House** by Sterling North (Random House, 1987).

Prewriting

Explain that the prewriting activity will help students plan the content of their chapters on Abe Lincoln for the class book about U.S. presidents.

Writing

Remind students that their chapters should include interesting facts and stories about Abe Lincoln.

Sharing

When students have finished the writing activity, organize them into pairs. Have students in each pair edit each other's reports. Students should point out to each other what they find interesting and what they think could be improved. Pairs can then share their chapters with other students.

What Could and Could Not Really Happen

Distinguishing Fantasy from Reality

The ability to distinguish reality from fantasy requires readers to critically analyze and evaluate text. Being able to distinguish reality from fantasy is closely tied with readers' abilities to make connections and comparisons between what they read and what they already know to be true or possible. By developing these critical-thinking skills, students prepare for future reading experiences in which they will read critically to distinguish fact from opinion or to evaluate how language is used to influence and persuade.

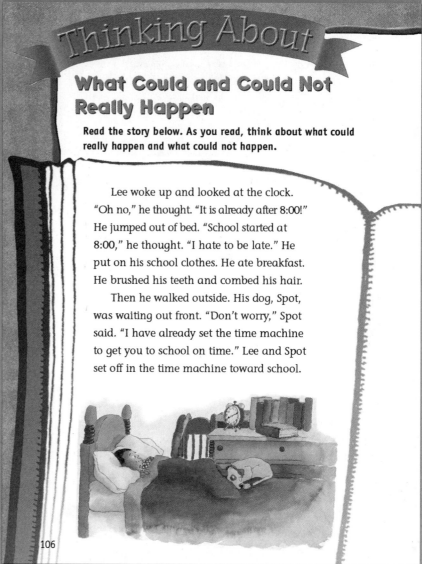

Thinking About

What Could and Could Not Really Happen

Read the story below. As you read, think about what could really happen and what could not happen.

> Lee woke up and looked at the clock. "Oh no," he thought. "It is already after 8:00!" He jumped out of bed. "School started at 8:00," he thought. "I hate to be late." He put on his school clothes. He ate breakfast. He brushed his teeth and combed his hair.
>
> Then he walked outside. His dog, Spot, was waiting out front. "Don't worry," Spot said. "I have already set the time machine to get you to school on time." Lee and Spot set off in the time machine toward school.

106

Introducing the Strategy

Write two headings on the chalkboard: "Movies, TV shows, or stories that could really happen" and "Movies, TV shows, or stories that could not really happen." Then ask students to name movies, TV shows, and stories and tell under which heading they should be placed. As students suggest titles, ask them to discuss how they know that the movie, TV show, or story goes in that column.

Applying the Strategy

Ask students to follow along as you read the story in the pupil book, or have a volunteer read it. Tell them to think about what could and could not happen as they read the story.

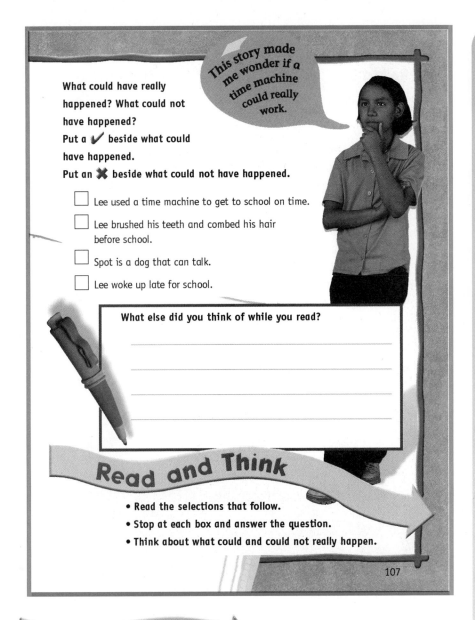

What could have really happened? What could not have happened?

Put a ✔ beside what could have happened.

Put an ✖ beside what could not have happened.

☐ Lee used a time machine to get to school on time.

☐ Lee brushed his teeth and combed his hair before school.

☐ Spot is a dog that can talk.

☐ Lee woke up late for school.

This story made me wonder if a time machine could really work.

What else did you think of while you read?

_____

_____

_____

_____

Read and Think

• Read the selections that follow.

• Stop at each box and answer the question.

• Think about what could and could not really happen.

107

Read and Think

• Remind students that answering the questions in the boxes will help them think about the selections.

• Encourage them to think about what could and could not really happen as they read the selections.

• Tell them that asking themselves questions such as, "Could this really happen?" and "Is this true?" can help them as they read.

Have students complete the questions independently or as a group. Review each sentence and discuss how students knew if it could or could not have happened.

Ask students what they were thinking about while the story was read. Have students elaborate on their responses if the connection with the text is not clear.

Explain to students that they will use this strategy as they read the selections in this unit.

Wilbur Meets the Thing

Strategy Focus

Distinguishing fantasy from reality.

Story at a Glance

A young monster and a little girl finally meet after being frightened by each other at night.

Vocabulary

You may want to introduce the following words to your students:

nonsense   *imagining*
grumbled   *snuggled*

Getting Students Started

• Introducing the Selection

Ask students if they have ever been scared of noises at night. What have they thought they were hearing? Why do they think that people seem to get more frightened at night and in the dark? Tell students that they are going to read a story about someone else who gets scared at night.

• Purpose for Reading

Students read to find out what it is that Wilbur hears.

Wilbur Meets the Thing

By Caroline Coderre

This selection is about Wilbur, who gets scared at night. Wilbur decides to find out what is making the noises he hears when he is tucked in bed. Read the selection to find out what Wilbur hears.

Wilbur was scared.

He was tucked safely into bed for the night, and all was dark and cozy.

But . . .

"Mom!" Wilbur called. "There's something out there!" His eyes were round with fear.

> **1** What does Wilbur think is out there?

108

Possible Responses
Question 1

Probably a robber.
This is a valid guess given the context of the story.

A monster under the bed.
This is a realistic response that reflects typical childhood fears and shows that the student understands the story.

He doesn't know.
This is a good response that shows the student is understanding the story. To encourage creative thinking, ask, "What might he be afraid is out there?"

"Nonsense," said his mother. "You're imagining it. Go to sleep."

Wilbur huddled deeper in bed and pulled his blanket up to his chin. He was sure he could hear the thing out there moving.

"Mom," he called again. "It's still there. I can hear it."

"Really, Wilbur," his mother said, sighing. "I told you, you're imagining things. There's nothing there. Now please be quiet and go to sleep."

 2 If you were Wilbur, what would you say to your mother?

109

Possible Responses
Question 2

Can I sleep in your bed?

I'm too scared to be quiet.

These responses show comprehension of the story and demonstrate an ability to identify with the main character. This identification with a character or events in a story is an important way that students become engaged with the stories they read.

I don't know.

As the students write, encourage them to try to respond to the question in the box. However, if students are having trouble answering the question, encourage them to write whatever the story inspires them to think about. Ask this student, "How would you feel if you were Wilbur?"

To help strengthen students' comprehension of the story, have them use a colored marker to highlight the parts of the story where there are clues that Wilbur is the monster and the "thing" is a child.

"I wish she'd believe me," Wilbur grumbled to himself. "It's not fair. That thing is out there every night, keeping me awake. If I could catch it, then Mom would HAVE to believe me."

Wilbur grabbed his fishing net. With his furry, green hand he pushed open the door of the closet where he lived. "Here goes!" he thought.

 3 What just happened?

"Grroarr!" roared Wilbur as he leaped out into the middle of the bedroom.

"Eek!" yelled the child on the bed, sitting up.

"Aak!" yelled Wilbur. "You scared me."

"YOU scared ME," cried the girl. "I knew there was a monster in the closet. Mom didn't believe me."

 4 Draw a picture of Wilbur and the thing that he heard outside of his bed.

110

Possible Responses

Question 3

He is the monster!
This response shows a high level of comprehension. The student has understood the surprise twist in the story—that Wilbur is actually the monster and the "thing" is a child.

Why is his hand green?
This response shows some confusion about the text, but does demonstrate an understanding of reality versus fantasy. The student recognizes that if Wilbur is a child then his hand should not be green. Encourage the student to continue reading to see if the story becomes clearer.

Question 4

Student artwork should reflect the characters in the story: Wilbur should be depicted as a furry green monster, perhaps with a fishing net, and the child is a girl in bed.

"My mom didn't believe me either," said Wilbur. "What's your name?"

"Lisa," said the girl. "You don't look so scary close up. Your fur looks soft."

"My name's Wilbur," said the little monster. "You're not as big as I thought."

"Do you eat people?" asked Lisa.

"No!" cried Wilbur. "Yuck! I like peanut butter sandwiches, apples, bananas, things like that. I hate spinach, though."

"Ugh. Me, too," said Lisa. "That's a nice fishing net you have."

"You could borrow it sometime," offered Wilbur.

"Do you sleep in my closet?" Lisa asked.

"Every night," said Wilbur. "I'm sorry I scared you."

> **5** How is Wilbur like other monsters? How is he different from other monsters?

(111)

Reinforcing the Strategies

This selection works well for reinforcing the strategy of making and revising predictions. For example, encourage students to predict what might happen in the story by stopping students midway and asking them to write what they think might happen next. At the end of the story students could share their responses and compare them with the actual ending of the story.

Possible Responses
Question 5

Would a monster be so nice?
It seems clear that this student's background knowledge about monsters is making him or her skeptical about how nice Wilbur is portrayed in the story. Challenging the text in this way shows that the student understands and is thinking about the story.

He was scared too! Remember?
This student does not explicitly say that other monsters aren't scared, and Wilbur is different because he is scared. However, this is an implied point. To encourage the student to clarify his or her response, ask, "Does Wilbur's fear make him different from other monsters?"

Monsters are big.
This student may be confused by the question or the story, or may be challenging what has been presented in the text about monsters. Ask this student, "Is Wilbur big or little? Does this make him alike or different from monsters that you know about?"

It is very important to have the students read and discuss what they have written in the boxes about the elements of fantasy and reality in the story.

Discussing the Think-Alongs

- Give as many students as possible a chance to tell what they wrote in one of the boxes.
- Have students explain what they were thinking when they wrote.
- Ask students how they are able to distinguish what is real from what is not real.

Reteaching

For those students who have not written or are having difficulty with the activity:

- Ask them to tell what they were thinking about as they read.
- Model your thought process in distinguishing fantasy from reality as you read.
- Ask questions that motivate the students to think about the elements of fantasy and reality in the story, such as the following:
  - *Who did you think Wilbur was when you started reading?*
  - *Have you ever felt like Wilbur did?*
  - *When Wilbur opened the closet door, what was the surprise in the story?*

"I'm sorry I scared you, too. I'd better go to sleep now. See you tomorrow?"

"I'll be here," said Wilbur. "Shall I tuck you in?"

Wilbur smoothed the covers over the little girl. Then he bent down and kissed her cheek. "Good night," he said.

"I'm glad you sleep in my closet," said Lisa. "It's nice to have a friend close by in the dark."

"Yes, it is," said Wilbur. Then Wilbur the monster went back into the closet, and Lisa the little girl snuggled down under the covers, and they both went to sleep.

> 6 Would you like to have Wilbur live in your closet?

112

Possible Responses
Question 6

He tucks her into bed.
This response does not directly answer the question, although one might infer that the student sees this as a positive result of having Wilbur live in the closet. Ask this student, "Is this something that you would like?"

Maybe if he didn't come out.
This is a valid response that reflects both the student's discomfort with monsters and a close reading of the story. To encourage this student to make-believe, ask, "What do you think it would be like if you had a monster in your closet who never came out?" or "What would you do when you had to get your clothes?"

My closet is already too full.
This student shows an understanding of fantasy versus reality by incorporating real-world concerns into the response to this question. Encourage this student to make-believe that there was room in the closet and Wilbur might live there. Ask, "Now would you want Wilbur to live there?"

Time to Write!

"Wilbur Meets the Thing" is fun to read. It is a story with a twist. Now, you are going to write your own story.

- For this activity, you will write a story including things that could and could not really happen.

Prewriting

First, think about what you are going to write. Who will the characters in your story be? What will happen in your story?

Draw a picture of a character in your story.

About my story character: _____

_____

What happens to my story character: _____

_____

_____

Writing

Now, use another sheet of paper to write your story.

113

Making Connections

Activity Links

- Have students read mystery stories or other stories with surprise endings.
- As a class, generate a list of monsters (with Wilbur first on the list) that the students have read or heard about. Then, discuss how these monsters are different from each other. Discuss what makes a monster a monster, and ask, "If there are so many differences, what do monsters have in common?"
- Ask students to draw pictures of different monsters. Alternatively, ask students to draw things that they have imagined are hiding in their closets or under their beds. Have students share their drawings with the class and discuss how the drawings reflect the difference between fantasy and reality.

Reading Links

You might want to include books from these series in a discussion of mysteries:

- **The Encyclopedia Brown Series** by Donald J. Sobol (Bantam Skylark).
- **The Baby-Sitters Club Mystery Series** by Ann M. Martin (Apple).
- **The Goosebumps Series** by R. L. Stine (Apple).
- **The Arthur Adventures Series** by Marc Tolon Brown (Little Brown & Co.).
- **Steck-Vaughn Mystery, Adventure, and Science Fiction Series** (Steck-Vaughn Company, 1995).

Prewriting

Tell students that the prewriting exercise will help them plan their stories. Tell students that one of the first steps in planning a story is to pick a main character. Another important step is developing a plot (planning what will happen in the story).

Writing

Remind students that they should write a make-believe story that they would like to share with the class.

Sharing

Have volunteers read their make-believe stories to the rest of the class. Ask the class to discuss what could really happen in each story and what could not happen.

Save the River!

Strategy Focus

Distinguishing fantasy from reality.

Story at a Glance

A boy and his computer travel back in time to help two friends save a river.

Vocabulary

You may want to introduce the following words to your students:

relatives   *polluting*
aide   *article*
conserve

Getting Students Started

• *Introducing the Selection*

Ask students if there is anything they would like to change in their town or community. Discuss the idea that individuals can make a difference, and brainstorm some ideas of how students could make a difference where they live. Tell students that they're going to be reading a story about a boy named Vince who lives 100 years in the future with his computer, Jane. In the story, Vince and Jane travel back in time to help save a river.

• *Purpose for Reading*

Students read to find out how the children in the story save the river.

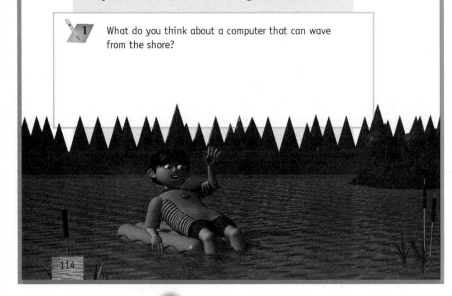

Save the River!

By Sarah Glasscock

This selection is about a boy named Vince. He lives in the future with his computer named Jane. They go back in time to help save a river. Read the selection to find out how they try to save the river.

A River in Trouble

It was the year 2097. Vince was floating on his back in the clear water of the San Carlos River. His computer named Jane was waving from the shore.

1   What do you think about a computer that can wave from the shore?

114

Possible Responses
Question 1

That can't really happen.
In this response, the student is clearly distinguishing fantasy from reality.

I wish I had that computer!
This student is making a personal connection with the material. You might ask the student what use he or she would have for such a computer.

How does it do that?
This response indicates curiosity as well as a good understanding of the text.

"Jane, would you show me what this river looked like one hundred years ago?" Vince asked.

"Sure. Why do you want to see it as it was back then?" asked Jane.

"I'd just like to know if the river was this beautiful then," said Vince.

2 What are you thinking about now?

115

Strategy Tip

Remind students to think about the difference between fantasy and reality as they read. Stories like "Save the River!" may have elements of fantasy, but they also teach some real-life lessons.

Possible Responses
Question 2

I saw an old picture of where I live.

The "What are you thinking about now?" questions prompt students to use a variety of reading strategies. This response shows the student making a personal connection with the situation described in the story.

I'd like to see back in time.

This response shows a personal connection with the text and a desire to visualize past events.

This sounds pretty.

This student is clearly visualizing the scene described in the story. Visualizing is a strategy that good readers use to understand what they are reading.

Soon Jane's screen lit up. There was a picture of the river as it had looked one hundred years ago. Jane made the picture bigger so Vince could see it.

Vince looked closely and saw a man and his son fishing. "Maybe that's my great-great grandfather!"

Jane quickly searched her computer memory. "That could be. You did have relatives here at that time."

"There were so many animals that came to the river back then," Jane said. "The San Carlos has been giving them food and water for hundreds of years."

A few feet away, Vince saw a deer drinking from the river. "It still does. The river hasn't changed. That's amazing. I wonder why the river hasn't changed."

116

ESOL

Organize students into pairs. Pair students acquiring English with fluent English speakers. Ask students to take turns retelling the story in their own words to their partners. Have students make a list of unfamiliar words to look up in the dictionary.

A message popped up on Jane's screen from May 5, 1997. It said, "Help us save the river! Lina and Al." The words kept flashing on the screen.

"Jane, we have to do something!" said Vince. "Since you and I can travel back in time, let's go back and help them."

3 What books or movies does this remind you of?

Jane agreed that they should travel back into the past and see the river as it was back in 1997.

Jane sent a message to get the time machine. Suddenly the Time Traveler, a big bubble ship, floated down to the ground. "Get ready for a trip, Jane. Let's travel back in time to the year 1997," said Vince.

"If we go back, we can't change things ourselves," Jane reminded him. "We can only help Lina and Al."

Vince said, "I know, but let's try to help them." Vince and Jane changed into 1997 clothes and got into the Time Traveler. Then it rose into the sky and began its journey back in time.

117

Possible Responses
Question 3

....

I read a book like this where the kids traveled in time.

> This student uses personal experience to relate to the text.

My mom read me a story called "The Lion, the Witch, and the Wardrobe."

> This student responds to the question directly. Encourage the student to elaborate by explaining why "Save the River!" reminds her or him of *The Lion, the Witch, and the Wardrobe.*

We have a computer at home but it can't talk.

> This student does not respond directly to the question, but does make a connection to the story. The student also recognizes that the computer in the story is different from the computer that he or she has at home. Redirect by asking whether the story reminds him or her of any books or movies.

Vince and Jane to the Rescue

The Time Traveler landed by some homes near the San Carlos River. But the year was 1997! Vince and Jane heard some voices outside. They peeked out and saw a girl and a boy talking to a woman. Jane quickly did a computer check on them. "It's Lina and Al!" Jane said.

 4   What do you think Vince and Jane are going to do?

The woman was saying, "I don't agree with you. I don't want to give up my green grass and flowers. I don't want to see dried up grass when I look at my yard!"

Lina said, "Mom, if we use too much water, the San Carlos River could dry up someday." Lina's mom pointed the hose at her car to wash it.

Al pointed to some bags of lawn food. He asked, "Mrs. Reyna, are you going to put all that on your lawn?"

118

Possible Responses
Question 4

I guess rescue the other kids.
This response makes a prediction but shows a misunderstanding of events in the story. To help clarify, ask, "Do the kids need to be rescued, or do they need help saving the river?"

Help the river because it might get dirty.
This response indicates a good understanding of the story, makes a prediction, and reflects strong critical thinking skills.

fix everything
The response shows an understanding of the story, but is vague. Ask, "What problem do you think Vince and Jane will try to fix?"

"Yes, green grass needs lots of food and water," Lina's mom said. "It doesn't grow on its own. I'm just trying to make our home look beautiful. Don't worry so much. Nothing bad is going to happen to the river."

"But the lawn food goes into the ground, and it ends up in the river," Al said.

"And the soapy water from the car ends up in the river, too," Lina said.

"What do you want me to do?" Lina's mom asked. "Drive a dirty car? Kill the grass? Let the weeds grow? I really don't think I'm polluting the river."

5   What do you think about what is happening to the river?

Possible Responses
Question 5

I don't think washing the car is that bad for the river.

This response states a personal opinion that challenges the story. Encourage such responses because being a critical reader includes questioning the text.

At my house we take the cans and the paper out.

This response reflects personal experience but does not seem immediately related to the question or to the story. Ask the student to explain what he or she is thinking.

This may prompt an explanation that reveals the comment to be thoughtful and relevant.

I don't know why she doesn't listen to the kids because the river sounds so pretty.

This response demonstrates the use of several different reading strategies, including questioning the text, making a personal connection, and visualizing the scene described in the story.

"We could take our car to a car wash that uses very little water," Lina said. "And our lawn doesn't need tons of water either, Mom."

"You're our mayor," Al added. "People will listen to you if you ask them to start SAVING water."

"You could ask people to work to keep the river clean," said Lina.

Mrs. Reyna aimed the hose at her car. "I'll think about it. You two go and play. Have some fun."

Lina and Al left and started walking down the sidewalk. Vince and Jane ran to catch them. They knew no one would understand that they had come from the future. So they had to act like they were from 1997.

---

6 What are you thinking about now?

Possible Responses
Question 6

I don't know how you'd act like that.

This response is probably questioning what Vince and Jane would do to act like they were from 1997. This student is demonstrating curiosity and an understanding of the text.

There's no way the computer could look like a kid.

This response demonstrates an understanding of the differences between fantasy and reality. By questioning the text, the student is also demonstrating critical thinking skills.

I wonder what people in the future would be like.

This student is comprehending and questioning the text as he or she reads. The student is making a thoughtful inference—that if Vince and Jane had to act like they were from 1997, people in the future must behave differently from people living in present times.

Vince said, "Hi. We got the message you sent about saving the river."

"How did you get it?" asked Al.

"We saw it on our computer. We want to help you save the San Carlos River," Vince added. "How can we help you?"

Lina shook her head. "Thanks, but I don't know. We're having a hard time getting people to listen to us. They can't see what they're doing to the river."

"What if people could see what they are doing to the river?" asked Vince. "They may not believe you now, but we could show them proof. Let's get some water from the river and put it in these jars. Then anyone will be able to see that the river water is dirty. We'll take the jars to a TV station. We can ask if they'll do a news story about the river."

Reinforcing the Strategies

This selection works well for reviewing the strategy of comparing and contrasting. After students have finished reading, have them make a list of how Vince's time is different from present times—for example, time travel and talking computers. Then, ask students to share their lists with the class.

"Wow, then people really will see what they're doing to the river. This idea might work," said Lina and Al.

"Then we could ask people to call the mayor with ideas about saving the river," Vince added.

"She's my mom," Lina said. "We're trying to think of a way to get her to change her mind. She thinks nothing bad will happen to the river."

"If enough people call, maybe she'll change her mind," said Vince. "It's worth a try."

They ran to the river with the jars. Vince filled them with some dirty river water. Then he put the lids on tightly.

 7 What do you think about their plan to save the river?

Possible Responses
Question 7

Is the water in the river that dirty?

How are they going to get the jar to be on TV?

Both of these students are thinking critically about the children's plan. These responses also demonstrate that a question can be an appropriate response to the questions in this activity.

I think the mom is going to listen to them now.

This response makes a prediction and shows an understanding of cause and effect.

The Mayor's Turn

Mayor Reyna was working in her office at the city hall. People had been calling her all morning. Jim Reed from the TV station was coming to talk to her.

Someone had put a jar of dirty water on her desk. Mayor Reyna held the jar up to the light and looked at the dirty water. The label on the jar said, "San Carlos River."

The mayor's aide, Bev, walked into the office. "Did you see this article in the newspaper today? It's about how dirty the water is in the San Carlos River. Everybody wants to talk to you about it," Bev said.

"Good," the mayor said with a smile. "I have a lot to say about it. Call the newspapers and the TV stations. Call Lina and Al, too. Ask them to come over. They'll be surprised at what I have to say."

8 What do you think the surprise will be?

123

Possible Responses
Question 8

She's going to help with the river.

She is going to show everybody the dirty water.

Both of these responses make predictions that are supported by the events in the story, and show good comprehension of what is being read.

Maybe she is going to find out about the kids from the future.

This prediction is inaccurate but clearly demonstrates comprehension of the story and shows that the student is thinking about what he or she is reading. In addition, the student's deduction seems plausible, for finding out about Vince and Jane's mission would underline the seriousness of saving the river.

It is very important to have the students read and discuss what they have written in the boxes to help them focus on the differences between fantasy and reality in the story.

Discussing the Think-Alongs

- Give as many students as possible a chance to tell what they wrote in one of the boxes.
- Have students explain what they were thinking when they wrote.
- Ask students how they are able to distinguish what is real from what is not real.

Reteaching

For those students who have not written or are having difficulty with the activity:

- Ask them to tell what they were thinking about as they read.
- Model your own reading to show how you distinguish fantasy from reality.
- Ask questions that prompt students to think about the elements of fantasy and reality in the story, such as the following:
- *What happened in the story that could not happen in real life?*
- *What happened in the story that could happen in real life?*
- *What happened in the story that does not happen today, but might happen in the near future?*

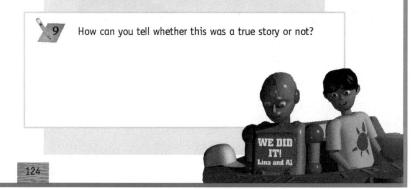

Many people came into the mayor's office. Mayor Reyna held up the jar of dirty water. "This is water from the San Carlos River. Would you drink this water? Would you swim in it? We must stop polluting this river now."

The mayor went on, "This is what we need to do. We'll do three things:

1. Conserve our water.
2. Stop polluting.
3. Learn to take care of the river.

I'm sure I can count on all of you to help save the river." Everyone clapped after the mayor's speech.

Vince and Jane said good-bye to Lina and Al. Then they sneaked back to the Time Traveler. It was time to go back to the future, to the year 2097. Vince said, "I'll miss Lina and Al. I think we helped them at just the right time."

Suddenly, a message trailed across Jane's screen. It said, "WE DID IT! Lina and Al."

9 How can you tell whether this was a true story or not?

Possible Responses
Question 9

It couldn't be true because those kids came in a time machine.

I don't think computers could really talk.

Both of these responses answer the question by selecting one element that shows that the story must be imaginary. Each response demonstrates that there is no right answer to the questions in this activity.

The part about the river seemed sort of true but then they wouldn't have gotten help from future people.

This response demonstrates a high level of understanding of the elements of fantasy and reality in this story.

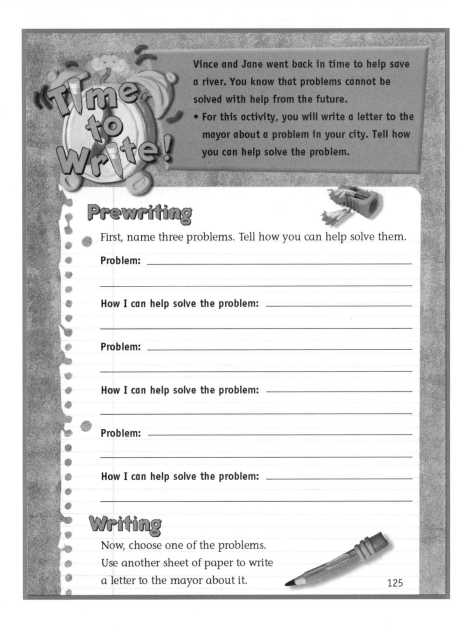

Time to Write!

Vince and Jane went back in time to help save a river. You know that problems cannot be solved with help from the future.
• For this activity, you will write a letter to the mayor about a problem in your city. Tell how you can help solve the problem.

Prewriting

First, name three problems. Tell how you can help solve them.

Problem: _____

_____

How I can help solve the problem: _____

_____

Problem: _____

_____

How I can help solve the problem: _____

_____

Problem: _____

_____

How I can help solve the problem: _____

_____

Writing

Now, choose one of the problems.
Use another sheet of paper to write
a letter to the mayor about it.

125

Making Connections

Activity Links

• Help students organize a campaign to carry out the project they voted on after sharing their letters.
• Discuss environmental issues such as recycling, endangered species, and rainforest deforestation. Have students research these topics in the library.
• Talk about citizenship and what it means to be a good citizen. Create a "good citizen" board on which students can both post their goals for volunteering in the school or community and chart their progress.

Reading Links

You might want to include the following books in a discussion about community service or the environment:
• **Deep in the Forest series** by Saviour Pirotta (Raintree Steck-Vaughn, 1999).
• **The Kid's Guide to Service Projects: Over 500 Service Ideas for Young People Who Want to Make a Difference** by Barbara A. Lewis and Pamela Espeland (Free Spirit Publishers, 1995).
• **The Lorax (Classic Seuss)** by Dr. Seuss (Random House, 1998).

Prewriting

Tell students that the prewriting activity will help them plan what they are going to write. If students have trouble generating a list of things they could do to help their community, the class can brainstorm topics before writing. These might include volunteering at the local animal shelter, gathering recyclable materials, cleaning a vacant lot, helping an elderly neighbor with yard work, or serving meals at a homeless shelter.

Writing

Tell students that they should choose only one problem to discuss in their letters to the mayor. Explain that focusing on one problem will allow them to explore their topic more fully. In addition, suggest that their letters first describe the problem and then discuss possible solutions.

Sharing

Have volunteers share and discuss their letters with the class. Afterward, poll the students to discover which project they would most like to carry out.

Strategy Focus

Distinguishing fantasy from reality.

Story at a Glance

A young tiger helps all tigers get their proper coat.

Vocabulary

You may want to introduce the following words to your students:

clattering   *ridiculous*
mumbled   *snapped*
mistake

Getting Students Started

· Introducing the Selection

Ask students if they know any folktales or fables about why things are the way they are. Perhaps students have read stories about how the leopard got its spots or where the moon and the stars came from. Many cultures have their own folktales or fables to explain events in the natural world. Tell students that they are about to read a story about why tigers have stripes.

· Purpose for Reading

Students read to learn how tigers got their stripes.

Some Jungles Are Noisier Than Others

By J.R.M. Vance

 **Let's Read**

Have you ever wondered why some animals look the way they do? This selection tells how tigers might have looked. Read the selection to find out how tigers got their stripes.

Long ago, tigers were not covered with a coat of stripes. No, back then tigers were covered with small metal pipes. I know that sounds silly, but it's true. Those pipes made an awful noise, clattering and clanging throughout the jungle. The tigers were not happy about their coats, but they did not know how to change them.

1 What do you think about tigers with pipes?

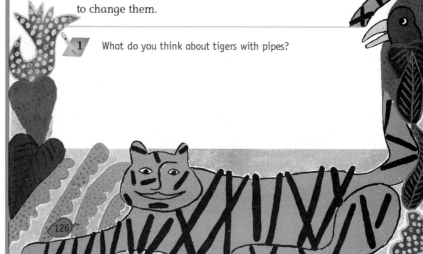

126

Possible Responses
Question 1

How did the pipes get on there?

> This response shows an understanding of the text and reveals critical thinking about the origin of an unlikely detail.

That must have been really noisy.

> This response shows comprehension of the text as well as a vivid imagining of the details of the story.

Couldn't they have just cut them off?

> This response not only questions the text, but goes a step further in proposing a solution to the tigers' problem.

One day a young tiger decided that he had had quite enough of his coat of pipes. He went deep into the jungle, and he found Sahr, the Giver of Large-Cat Coats.

"Hello," said the tiger. "My name is Tonga, and I would like to have a coat that is not covered with pipes."

Sahr blinked the sleep from his eyes. "I really can't see what I can do for you. Things are the way they are supposed to be. You must just learn to live with it." He closed his eyes again.

2 What are you thinking about now?

127

Strategy Tip

Remind students to think about what could really happen and what could not really happen as they read.

Possible Responses
Question 2

. . . .

He's not very nice.

He's pretty lazy.

As both of these responses demonstrate, one of the ways that readers engage with a text is by stating a personal opinion about the characters.

That is sort of a funny name for the coat giver.

This response shows an understanding of humor in the text as well as the ability to distinguish a real name from an imaginary one.

To reinforce an understanding of the story's main events, have students draw pictures of the tigers at the beginning and at the end of the story. Then, have them explain how the pictures differ from each other.

"But this is ridiculous," said Tonga. "No one can sit and talk with us tigers because we make so much noise. There must have been a mistake."

"A mistake!" said Sahr, sitting up. "No, no, no, I never make mistakes. Now go away." Sahr lay back down and closed his eyes once more.

After a few minutes Sahr opened one eye and saw Tonga still sitting patiently beside him.

"Shoo," said Sahr. "Go away."

Tonga lay down and, as he did, his coat of pipes made so much noise Sahr had to cover his ears. "I'm not going away until you do something about my coat," said Tonga.

Sahr sighed. "Oh, all right," he said. "I'll look it up."

He opened up the bottom of the tree and searched around. After several minutes he pulled out a large moss-covered book.

"It's really not fair that I have to do so much work," grumbled Sahr. "Not fair at all."

3 What are you thinking about now?

128

Possible Responses
Question 3

•••

It's not like he is doing that much work.

If he made the mistake then he is the one who should fix it.

Both of these students are expressing an opinion and are showing a critical reading of the story.

Tonga's just going to keep waiting.

This response shows an understanding of the character of Tonga and offers a prediction.

Tonga waited.

"Hmm-hmm-hmm," said Sahr. "This is going to take me quite a long time. Tiger does begin with *T*, you know. It will take me awhile to get there. You had better come back next week."

Tonga said nothing. He just waited.

"Oh, drats," said Sahr, who was really quite lazy. "Let's see. Cougars, leopards, lions. Ah, here we are—tigers. You can see for yourself—right beside 'tigers' it says 'pipes.'"

Tonga looked. "That says 'stripes'!" exclaimed Tonga. "Not 'pipes.'"

4 What do you think about Sahr's mistake?

Possible Responses
Question 4

I made a mistake like that once when I was reading something.
This student makes a personal connection by comparing an event in the story with an experience that he or she has had. Ask, "What was your mistake?"

Stripes don't look like pipes.
Although this response reflects confusion about the facts of the story, it does show an attempt at critical thinking. To redirect the student's line of thought, you might ask, "Do you think the word stripes looks like the word pipes?"

What about all the other animals?
This student seems to be questioning other mistakes that Sahr might have made in giving out coats. The response shows a good understanding of the text and reveals strong critical thinking skills.

It is very important to have students discuss what they have written in the boxes to help them focus on distinguishing fantasy from reality.

Discussing the Think-Alongs

- Give as many students as possible a chance to tell what they wrote in one of the boxes.
- Ask students to explain what they were thinking when they wrote their responses.
- Have students explain how writing their thoughts helped them think about the story.

Reteaching

For those students who have not written or are having difficulty with the activity:

- Ask them to tell what they were thinking about as they read.
- Model how you distinguish fantasy from reality as you read.
- Ask questions that prompt students to think about the elements of fantasy and reality in the story, such as the following:

- *What happened in the story that could not happen in real life?*
- *How do you know that these events could not happen in real life?*
- *What happened in the story that might happen in real life?*

"Oh, my stars," said Sahr. He looked more closely at his book. "So it does." He laughed. "My mistake. Oh dear. Well, we had better fix that."

Sahr snapped his fingers, and instantly Tonga's coat of pipes was gone. Instead, he had a beautiful coat of stripes. Tonga thanked Sahr, and he raced off to find his friends.

Sahr lay back down and closed his eyes. "I really must be more careful," he mumbled sleepily. "It's like the time I covered all those leopards with pots."

As for Tonga and the other tigers, they thoroughly enjoyed their new coats, and the jungle became a much quieter place to live.

5 What are you thinking about now?

130

Possible Responses
Question 5

I bet that's not the real story of how tigers got their stripes because we learned it in science.

This student thoughtfully applies background knowledge and experience to distinguish between fantasy and reality.

I bet the stripes were better.

This response demonstrates an understanding of the text and an appropriate willingness to express an opinion.

I wonder if Sahr felt bad.

This response shows a connection to personal experience and reveals the ability to empathize. To encourage this, ask, "How would you feel if you had made that mistake?"

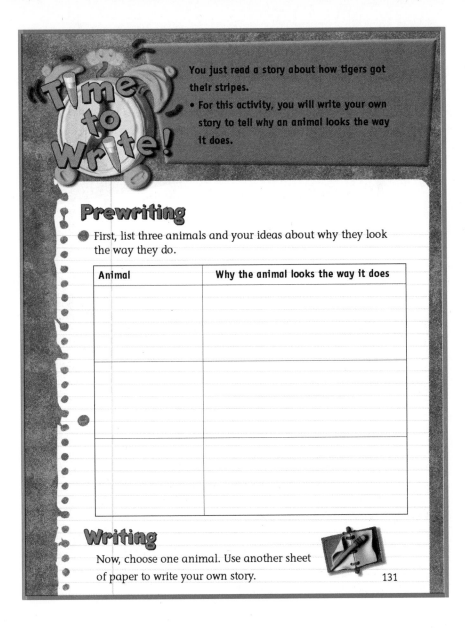

Time to Write!

You just read a story about how tigers got their stripes.

• For this activity, you will write your own story to tell why an animal looks the way it does.

Prewriting

First, list three animals and your ideas about why they look the way they do.

Animal	Why the animal looks the way it does

Writing

Now, choose one animal. Use another sheet of paper to write your own story.

131

Prewriting

Explain that the prewriting activity will help students decide upon an interesting theme for their story and help them organize their thoughts. You might want to encourage students to select animals with unusual features for their chart.

Writing

Remind students that their story should focus on how the animal came to look a particular way.

Sharing

When students finish the assignment, collect their stories in a class book.

Making Connections

Activity Links

• Share an origin tale for students to compare and contrast with "Some Jungles Are Noisier Than Others."

• Organize students into pairs or small groups. Give each group a folktale from a different culture to read and discuss. Ask each group to make a list of the elements of fantasy in their folktale.

• Explain to students that most folktales were first told by storytellers, rather than written down. Have students read their favorite folktales aloud to the class.

Reading Links

You might want to include the following books in a discussion about origin tales and folktales:

• **Favorite Folktales from Around the World** by Jane Yolen (Pantheon Books, 1988).

• **How Spiders Got Eight Legs** by Katherine Mead (Steck-Vaughn, 1998).

• **How the Rattlesnake Got Its Rattle** by Jeffrey Stoodt (Steck-Vaughn, 1998).

Thinking Along on Tests

The Tests

The next three selections are like standardized-test reading comprehension passages, with questions at the end of each selection. However, boxes with think-along questions appear within the selections to allow students to practice their think-along strategies.

Note that these selections are not designed to test specific reading strategies, but rather are designed to show students how thinking along will help them comprehend what they are reading and better answer questions about what they have read.

Introducing the Tests to Students

Remind students that this section is like the one that they completed earlier in the book. Tell them to apply the think-along process as they read the selections and then answer the questions at the end of each selection.

Thinking Along on Tests

You have been thinking along as you read. Now practice thinking along to help you answer test questions.

Read and Think

- Read each selection.
- Stop at each box and answer the question.
- Answer the questions at the end of each selection.

Why do bats have a bad name?

Bats have a bad name! Bats look scary to some people. Bats also can fly, but they are not birds. They are the only mammals that can fly. Some people are afraid that bats will get caught in their hair. Bats do not try to do that. Some people think bats will bite them. Bats almost never bite a person.

 1 What are you thinking about now?

Possible Responses
Question 1

I don't like bats.
This student is indicating a negative personal reaction to the topic. Such a response shows that the student is interacting with the text.

I saw a cartoon that had a vampire.
This response demonstrates a connection to personal experience.

I'm thinking about scary movies.
Again, this response shows a connection to personal experience and indicates comprehension of the text.

One kind of bat is called a vampire bat. Vampire bats do bite. But they bite cattle, not people. There are stories about people who become vampires. These horror stories are fun for people who like to be scared. They are just made up. They are not real. The fear of make-believe human vampires has helped give bats a bad name.

During the day bats hang upside down from the top of caves or rock piles. Bats sleep during the day and come out at night. This is another reason people are afraid of bats. People think bad things about the dark and night. They think that bats must be bad.

> **2** What are you thinking about now?

In some areas, people have tried to get rid of bats. They closed the caves where bats live. Bats could not leave to find food. They died without food. Bats have had a bad time.

"So what?" you might say. "So people should not be afraid of bats. Why is that important?" The important thing is that bats help people in many ways.

133

The Selections and Questions

The three selections in this test section are of different types: one fictional story and two expository articles. Each is followed by four multiple-choice questions and one short-answer question. The question format is typical of many standardized and criterion-referenced tests. The purpose-setting question format at the beginning of each selection is similar to that used on many nationally standardized tests. These questions help students to focus on a purpose for reading.

Possible Responses
Question 2

I saw some bats in a cave one time.
> This student is making a connection to personal experience.

Why don't they run into things?
> This is a good response that raises an issue not addressed by the text and indicates that the student is using critical thinking skills.

Sometimes you can't tell the difference between bats and birds at night.
> This student is using background knowledge and personal experience to facilitate comprehension.

Bats eat insects that harm crops and bite people. One bat can eat 1,000 mosquitoes in one hour! There is another good thing about bats. Bats that eat flowers help the flower make fruit. The bats also help move seeds to a new place to grow. Also, farmers use bat droppings, called guano, to help crops grow.

Today some people are trying to help bats. They want bats to eat insects. These people put bat houses in their yards. These houses have slots for the bats to climb in and sleep during the day. Some people turn on lights at night. They also plant flowers that bloom at night. Both of these attract moths and other insects that the bats like to eat. Bats also need water to drink. People make garden ponds for them.

It may take some time for everyone to understand that bats are not bad. It is important to spread the word about the good things that bats do.

 3 What are you thinking about now?

Possible Responses
Question 3

My grandpa has a bat house. They get in at the bottom.

This student is using personal experience and background knowledge to relate to the text.

I'm not afraid of them. I just don't like them.

This student is interacting with the text by expressing a personal reaction. You might encourage the student to gain a deeper understanding of his or her feelings by asking, "Why do you dislike bats?"

Why do people feed bats?

This student has addressed one of the main topics of the selection, but may have missed the point. Have the student reread the next-to-last paragraph, and then ask, "What does the paragraph say about why people feed bats?"

Darken the circle for the correct answer.

1. The writer thinks that people
   should _____.
   - Ⓐ get rid of all bats
   - Ⓑ stop reading about vampires
   - Ⓒ learn to like bats
   - Ⓓ live in caves

2. Some people are afraid that bats
   will bite and _____.
   - Ⓐ get caught in their hair
   - Ⓑ eat too many insects
   - Ⓒ hurt their ponds
   - Ⓓ harm crops

3. One fact about bats is that they
   _____.
   - Ⓐ try to bite people
   - Ⓑ sleep during the day
   - Ⓒ are birds
   - Ⓓ cannot fly

4. Bats help people because they
   _____.
   - Ⓐ live only in caves
   - Ⓑ like to scare people
   - Ⓒ have to drink water
   - Ⓓ eat many insects

Write your answer on the lines below.

5. What is one way people can help bats?

_____

_____

_____

_____

Answers and Analysis

1. C; inferential
2. A; literal
3. B; literal
4. D; literal
5. Literal.

Correct responses include any of the following details from the story:
- People can put bat houses in their yards.
- People can put lights in their yards to attract insects.
- People can plant flowers that bloom at night to attract insects.
- People can build ponds for bats to drink from.

Scoring Question 5:

2 = A meaningful and relevant response reflecting facts presented in the selection.
0 = A response that is a highly illogical suggestion, given the facts of the article.

Explanation of Comprehension Skills

Literal: The answer is specifically stated in the text.
Inferential: The answer can be inferred from the text, but it is not specifically stated.
Evaluative/Critical: The answer is based on an evaluation of the text.

Why does a hiker need a mirror?

Ashton had asked his friend Harrison to come along on his family's camping trip. The boys decided by the campfire that they would spend the next day hiking. Ashton suggested that his sister Tamesha could go along. Tamesha could see Harrison making a face even in the dark. Her mom and dad seemed to think it was a great idea.

The boys packed their backpacks before dark. They wanted to get an early start the next morning. Dad told Tamesha she could use the old pack he bought at the army-navy store. Tamesha was not sure what to take, so she left some of Dad's stuff in the bag.

 1   What are you thinking about now?

On the trail, Tamesha tried to keep up. They were climbing steep hills in places. Once or twice she got behind. "Hurry up!" Harrison growled. "You could have stayed at camp and gone fishing with your mom."

Possible Responses
Question 1

Something bad will happen if Tamesha goes.

This response makes a prediction. Encourage the student to read further to find out whether his or her prediction comes true.

Wouldn't it be too big for her? How old is she?

This student is questioning the facts of the story. These questions indicate that the student is developing strong critical thinking skills.

My uncle has one of those. It smells bad.

This response makes a connection to personal experience, expresses an opinion, and shows that the student is interacting with the text.

They stopped for lunch, and the boys pulled sandwiches out of their bags. "You did bring some food, didn't you?" Harrison said to Tamesha. He unwrapped his sandwich and winked at Ashton.

"No," Tamesha said. "I didn't think of that." She searched through Dad's backpack. She pulled a metal mirror out of a cloth. It caught the sun and shined in Harrison's eyes.

 2 What are you thinking about now?

"Gee, whiz!" Harrison growled. "Why did you bring a mirror on a hike?" Then he reached for another sandwich in his pack. "Your mom said this is for you," he said, handing it to her.

They hiked for hours. Tamesha thought they were going in circles. Finally, Ashton stopped. "I'm lost," he said. "I don't have any idea which way leads back to camp."

"*We're* lost, you mean," Harrison said. "We'd better figure it out, though. The sun will go down in a couple of hours."

137

Possible Responses
Question 2

. . . .

I'd just be mean back to Harrison. I don't like him.
This response indicates an understanding of the conflict in the story and expresses an opinion.

Maybe Harrison was right.
This response expresses an opinion about the story, but is vague. Ask, "What do you think Harrison is right about?"

Will Ashton share his lunch with Tamesha?
This prediction is inaccurate but reflects a good understanding of the characters. Encourage this student to look for the answer to his or her question in the next passages of the selection.

Tamesha was nervous. They were lost in the woods! Finally they came to the top of a bare hill where they could see a long way.

"Look!" Ashton yelled, pointing down at one valley. He could see his parents on a trail. They were looking for the hikers. The children began yelling to them. They could tell that they could not be heard.

Tamesha thought a minute. Then she pulled the mirror out of her dad's pack.

Harrison made an awful face. "Great!" he said. "What good will that do?"

Tamesha held the mirror so that it caught the sun and made bright flashes. Soon they could see Mom and Dad waving their arms at them.

"Sure glad you had that mirror, Tamesha," Harrison said, smiling.

3 What are you thinking about now?

Possible Responses
Question 3

Whose mom and dad are they?

This student might be confused about the details of the story. Ask, "Whose parents came on the camping trip?"

This is a good story. Harrison was wrong.

This response expresses an opinion and indicates that the reader is involved in the story.

I think they saw the flashes.

This response reveals a careful reading of the story. If some students need help understanding what Tamesha did with the mirror, explain how someone can angle a mirror to catch the sun and reflect its light in a certain direction. Because the flash could be seen from far away, it caught Mom and Dad's attention.

Darken the circle for the correct answer.

6. How does Tamesha know that Harrison does not want her to go along?
   - Ⓐ He makes a face.
   - Ⓑ He eats her sandwich.
   - Ⓒ He takes her mirror.
   - Ⓓ He smiles at her.

7. Tamesha brought the mirror because _____.
   - Ⓐ she wanted to look good
   - Ⓑ Ashton needed it
   - Ⓒ Harrison didn't like her having it
   - Ⓓ it was already in Dad's pack

8. Why were Mom and Dad out on the trail?
   - Ⓐ They were looking for the mirror.
   - Ⓑ They knew Tamesha had no sandwich.
   - Ⓒ They thought the children were lost.
   - Ⓓ They were on their way home.

9. A good title for this story would be _____.
   - Ⓐ Friendly Campers
   - Ⓑ Tamesha Saves the Day
   - Ⓒ Tamesha's Mistake
   - Ⓓ The Broken Mirror

Write your answer on the lines below.

10. How do you think Tamesha feels at the end of the story?

_____

_____

_____

_____

Answers and Analysis

6. A; inferential
7. D; inferential
8. C; inferential
9. B; evaluative/critical
10. Evaluative/critical.

Answers will vary. Possible responses include the following:

- She is probably happy not to be lost anymore.
- She is tired of Harrison but not sorry that she came on the hike.
- She might be hungry because she ate only one sandwich all day.
- She is very happy to show Harrison that she could rescue their group.

Scoring Question 10:

2 = A response describing a feeling that is consistent with the events in the story.
0 = A response that seems highly illogical given the facts of the story.

Explanation of Comprehension Skills

Literal: The answer is specifically stated in the text.
Inferential: The answer can be inferred from the text, but it is not specifically stated.
Evaluative/Critical: The answer is based on an evaluation of the text.

What do we know about Cliff Dwellers?

Do you know about the Cliff Dwellers? They are one of the great mysteries of the world. They built their homes into high, steep cliffs. Some ruins are over 2,000 feet above the floor of the valley below.

Many of these ruins are found in the southwestern United States. Here the four states Colorado, Utah, Arizona, and New Mexico meet. This area is called the "four corners." The most famous ruins are found on Mesa Verde. It is a high, flat-topped hill in Colorado.

No one knows for sure who built these cliff dwellings. Who were these people? Where did they come from? Where did they go? Many experts believe that these people were the ancestors of today's Pueblo Indians. The Pueblo call them the Anasazi.

1 What are you thinking about now?

Possible Responses
Question 1

Are Cliff Dwellers a people or a place?

This response shows confusion about the facts of the passage but also demonstrates that the student is questioning the text as he or she reads.

Anasazi sounds like the name of a alien on a show I saw. Maybe they were aliens.

This student is making a connection to personal experience and is using a lot of imagination.

This is kind of hard to get. Maybe it will get easier.

This student finds the reading challenging. Ask questions to facilitate comprehension, such as, "What kinds of homes did the Cliff Dwellers live in?" and "In what part of the country did they live?"

These people probably first dug holes, or pits, to store supplies. Later they lined the pits with stones, put on roofs, and moved in. Then they began to build their homes on ledges in the sides of the cliffs. No one knows why they did this. Maybe they moved to be safe from enemies.

Some of these cliff buildings were four stories high. The bottom floor had no doors or windows. People used a ladder to enter through a hole in the ceiling. They could then pull the ladder in behind them.

> **2** What are you thinking about now?

The cliff homes were built of stone and mud. One dwelling has over 200 rooms. It is called Cliff Palace. It had special rooms for keeping food and blankets for the winter.

There was a large room under the floor of the palace. It was the kiva (KEE vah). It was for special ceremonies, storytelling, and weaving. Only men could go down into the kiva. It had a deep, dark hole leading to what the people thought was the secret of life.

141

Possible Responses
Question 2

How can this be a mystery if they know this much?
This student is challenging the text while demonstrating a high level of understanding. Assessing material is crucial in becoming a critical reader.

I'd hate living in a hole.
This student shows some comprehension of the text by expressing an opinion.

Maybe they moved because there was a flood. We had to move when there was a flood.
This student is demonstrating a personal connection and is speculating about the reasoning behind actions mentioned in the text. This response shows a high degree of involvement with the text.

Women stayed above the kiva and made clay pots for cooking corn, squash, and beans. They grew these crops on the flat top of the hill above the dwelling. But this area could be very, very dry.

After about 300 years these people left their cliff homes. The reason is a mystery. Some experts believe there was too little rain, and the crops may have died.

Everything we know about the Cliff Dwellers we have guessed from the ruins of their homes. Yet the more we find, the more mysterious they seem.

 3 What are you thinking about now?

Possible Responses
Question 3

Maybe they just didn't want to be there anymore.
This response speculates about the Cliff Dwellers' motivations for leaving their homes. Drawing conclusions is a good reading strategy that shows a high level of interaction with the text.

time
This response is vague, but it may hold a deeper meaning for the student. Encourage him or her to elaborate and express the idea more clearly.

Where are the cliff people now?
This question reflects the fact that much about the Cliff Dwellers is unknown. If the passage leaves several students with questions, encourage the class to discuss the passage. Someone may want to volunteer to look for more information about the Cliff Dwellers. Point out that one way that reading helps people learn is by motivating them to look for answers on their own.

Darken the circle for the correct answer.

11. The Cliff Dwellers are so
mysterious because _____.

   Ⓐ they left no ruins

   Ⓑ little about them is known for
     certain

   Ⓒ they had no homes

   Ⓓ they grew no food

12. Some people believe the cliff
dwellings were built to
_____.

   Ⓐ get up above floods

   Ⓑ reach the sky

   Ⓒ be away from enemies

   Ⓓ find the secret of life

13. What is a mesa?

   Ⓐ a high flat-topped hill

   Ⓑ a hole in the ground

   Ⓒ something made of corn

   Ⓓ the story of the Anasazi

14. We have learned that the Cliff
Palace _____.

   Ⓐ was in a valley

   Ⓑ was built of pots

   Ⓒ had no place for food

   Ⓓ had many rooms

Write your answer on the lines below.

15. Describe the cliff dwellings.

_____

_____

_____

_____

143

Answers and Analysis

11. B; inferential
12. C; literal
13. A; inferential
14. D; literal
15. Literal.

Correct responses should include
any details from the selection, such
as the following:

- They were several stories high.
- They were made of stone and
  mud.
- The first floor had no windows
  or door, just a hole in the ceiling.
- They used a ladder to climb to
  the second floor.
- The rooms were big; one of
  them was used for special ceremonies.
- Some had many rooms.

Scoring Question 15:

2 = A good answer will clearly
review at least one fact about
the cliff dwellings from the
selection.

0 = A weak answer will not
review any detail clearly or will
state it incorrectly.

Explanation of Comprehension Skills

Literal: The answer is specifically stated in the text.

Inferential: The answer can
be inferred from the text, but
it is not specifically stated.

Evaluative/Critical: The
answer is based on an evaluation of the text.

Making Connections

Discussion

After the students have completed the questions for all
three selections, discuss with
them what they wrote in the
boxes. Ask students to tell
what they wrote in a box and
to explain why they wrote
what they did. Then, have
students discuss how writing
in the boxes helped them to
remember what the selection
was about so they could better answer the questions at
the end of the selection.

For your own curricular planning, you might also want to
review what students have
written in the boxes. Reading
what students have written
will give you an idea of how
well they are comprehending
what they read and whether
they need additional review
of the process of thinking
along as they read.

Scoring

Refer to the discussion of
test taking on page T11 of
the teacher's edition for
information on scoring and
interpreting student scores.

Acknowledgments

Grateful acknowledgment is made to the following authors and publishers for the use of copyrighted materials. Every effort has been made to obtain permission to use previously published material. Any errors or omissions are unintentional.

Abe Lincoln's Hat by Martha Brenner. Text copyright © 1994 by Martha Brenner. Illustrations copyright © 1994 by Donald Cook. Reprinted by arrangement with Random House, Inc.

Diego Rivera: An Artist's Life by Sarah Vázquez. Copyright © 1998 by Steck–Vaughn Company.

"Elsa's Pet" by Maureen Ash. Copyright © 1998 by Maureen Ash. First appeared in *Click* magazine, August 1998. Reprinted by permission of Maureen Ash.

Floss by Kim Lewis. Copyright © 1992 Kim Lewis. Reproduced by permission of Candlewick Press Inc., Cambridge, MA.

Gail Devers: A Runner's Dream by Katherine Mead. Copyright © 1998 by Steck–Vaughn Company.

A Look at Spiders by Jerald Halpern. Copyright © 1998 by Steck–Vaughn Company.

The Paper Bag Princess by Robert N. Munsch, illustrated by Michael Martchenko. Copyright © 1980 by Robert N. Munsch and Michael Martchenko. Reprinted by permission of Annick Press Ltd.

"Rocco's Yucky" by Linda Crotta Brennan. Reprinted by permission of LADYBUG magazine, November 1998, Vol. 9, No. 3, copyright © 1998 by Linda Crotta Brennan.

Save the River! by Sarah Glasscock. Copyright © 1998 by Steck–Vaughn Company.

"Some Jungles Are Noisier Than Others" by J. R. M. Vance. Copyright © 1995 by Highlights for Children, Inc., Columbus, Ohio. Reprinted by permission of Highlights for Children, Inc.

Whales: The Gentle Giants by Joyce Milton. Text copyright © 1989 by Joyce Milton. Illustrations copyright © by Alton Langford. Reprinted by arrangement with Random House, Inc.

"Wilbur Meets the Thing" by Caroline Coderre. Copyright © 1995 by Highlights for Children, Inc., Columbus, Ohio. Reprinted by permission of Highlights for Children, Inc.

Illustration Credits

Linda Kelen, pp.4, 28, 72, 106; Michael Martchenko, pp.6–12; Tadeusz Majewski, cover, pp.14–20; George Ulrich, cover, pp.22–26; Alton Langford, pp.30–40; Laura Jackson, pp.63–64, 69, 136; Kim Lewis, pp.74–80; Donald Cook, pp.94–104; Esther Szegedy, cover, pp.108–112; D. R. Greenlaw, cover, pp.114–124; Maya Itzna–Brooks, cover, pp.126–130.

Photography Credits

Cover (front) Sam Dudgeon; cover (back) ©Steven Raymer; p.T4 ©Jeff Dunn/Stock Boston; p.T5 ©Steven Raymer; p.T8(t) Cindy Ellis; p.T8(b) ©Ian Shaw/Tony Stone Images; pp.T12–T15, 5, 29 Rick Williams; p.42 ©Francis G. Mayer/Corbis; p.43 ©PhotoDisc; p.44 ©Nik Wheeler/Corbis; p.45 ©PhotoDisc; p.46 Danny Lehman/©Corbis; p.47 CORBIS/Archivo Iconografico, S.A.; p.48–49(t) The Detroit Institute of the Arts; p.48(b) ©PhotoDisc; p.50 Danny Lehman/©Corbis; p.52 ©Rocky Jordan/Animals Animals; p.53 ©Chris Mattison; Frank Lane Picture Agency/Corbis; p.54 ©Paul Freed/Animals Animals; p.55 ©Hal Horwitz/Corbis; p.56 ©Donald Specker/Animals Animals; p.57 ©Patti Murray/Animals Animals; p.58 ©Anthony Bannister; ABPL/Corbis; p.59 ©C. W. Perkins/Animals Animals; p.60 ©Ronnie Kaufman/The Stock Market; p.67 ©Corel Photo Studios; p.73 Rick Williams; p.82 ©Gary M. Prior/Allsport; p.83 ©Mike Powell/Allsport; p.84 ©Focus on Sports; p.85 ©Mike Powell/Allsport; p.86 ©Bob Daemrich; p.87 ©Steve Powell/Allsport; p.89 ©Allsport; p.90 ©Simon Bruty/Allsport; p.91 ©David Cannon/Allsport; p.92 ©Gary M. Prior/Allsport; p.107 Rick Williams; p.132 ©Raymond A. Mendez/Animals Animals; p.134 ©Dalton, S. OSF/Animals Animals; p.140 ©PhotoDisc; p.142 CORBIS/Richard A. Cooke.